WITHDRAWN

A VOICE IN THE BOX

BOB EDWARDS

A VOICE IN THE BOX

MY LIFE IN RADIO

THE UNIVERSITY PRESS OF KENTUCKY

Text illustrations by Susannah Edwards

THE UNIVERSITY PRESS OF KENTUCKY

Scholarly publisher for the Commonwealth, serving Bellarmine University, Berea College, Centre College of Kentucky, Eastern Kentucky University, The Filson Historical Society, Georgetown College, Kentucky Historical Society, Kentucky State University, Morehead State University, Murray State University, Northern Kentucky University, Transylvania University, University of Kentucky, University of Louisville, and Western Kentucky University. All rights reserved.

Editorial and Sales Offices: The University Press of Kentucky
663 South Limestone Street, Lexington, Kentucky 40508-4008

www.kentuckypress.com

15 14 13 12 11   5 4 3 2 1

Library of Congress Cataloging-in-Publication Data
Edwards, Bob, 1947–
A voice in the box : my life in radio / Bob Edwards.
p. cm.
Includes index.
ISBN 978-0-8131-3450-5 (hardcover : alk. paper) — ISBN 978-0-8131-3451-2 (ebook)
1. Edwards, Bob, 1947– 2. Radio broadcasters—United States—Biography. I. Title.
PN1991.4.E23
[A3 2011]
791.4402'8092—DC23
[B]

2011018440

THIS BOOK IS DEDICATED TO ANDY DANYO KUBIS AND
KEN GREENE. WHEN I NEEDED FRIENDS,
THEY WERE THERE.

CONTENTS

A VOICE IN THE BOX

REDEMPTION

———

November 6, 2004. Another cold, crisp night in the Windy City, but it's warm inside the Grand Ballroom of the Renaissance Chicago Hotel, where hundreds of radio royalty have gathered. Men in tuxedos and women in beautiful gowns or sexy cocktail dresses are clustered at thirty-four tables, each adorned with flowers and a burning candle. At one end of the ballroom is a bandstand, where Mickey and the Memories will entertain for everyone's dancing pleasure. That will come later, after dinner, many speeches, and a ceremony that is also a live radio program carried by the Premier group of stations.

The announcer is Jim Bohannon, one of my oldest friends in radio. He has alerted the diners to the Applause sign behind him and has let it be known that great audible enthusiasm is encouraged. At exactly 8:00 PM, we hear some upbeat theme music, and all respond to the sign's insistent demand for applause. A floor director cues Bohannon, who says, "Live, from Chicago, it's radio's biggest night—the 2004 Radio Hall of Fame induction ceremony. Tonight, the Radio Hall of Fame inducts XM Satellite Radio superstar Bob Edwards."

Superstar? We *do* love our hyperbole in radio. As of that night, my show on XM was just four weeks old. I doubt if the fellow who, months earlier, fired me from my previous show at NPR regarded me as anybody's superstar. But no matter—I was in the Hall.

Radio is closing in on its centennial, and its Hall of Fame includes the scientists who invented it, the hucksters who made money from it, the journalists who informed, the smart people who enlightened, and especially the enormously talented entertainers who came into our homes and cars and offices and made us laugh, cry, wince, fear, dread, guffaw, and enter worlds we could not imagine on our own. So here I am with Marconi, Edward R. Murrow, Arthur Godfrey, Alan Freed, Fibber McGee and Molly, Amos 'n' Andy, Orson Welles, Paul Harvey, Wolfman Jack, Bing Crosby, Gordon McLendon, Studs Terkel, Ma Perkins, Cousin Brucie, Red Barber, the Lone Ranger—just a stew of people, programs, and genres spanning generations and having nothing in common but the microphone and an audience.

My induction ceremony was a watershed event—the last in a series of traumas and triumphs that had kept me in a state of emotional whiplash for most of the year. So this night in Chicago was the end of something but also the beginning of something. It symbolized my passage to a new radio home and an environment in which I could do what I regard as the very best work of my career.

Induction really recognizes a much longer journey—the span of a career. So let's go back to the little burg where my radio journey began in 1968, when I had no notion of a hall of fame—only a burning desire to be a voice in the box.

LAUNCH

It was a perfect day for lust, a mild, sunny day in October 1968. The program director of the radio station had figured out a way to rendezvous with a female listener without his wife noticing he was not on the air. He preempted local programs, including his own, and carried ABC's national coverage of Apollo 7. The station had not shown such dedication to public service in the past, but his wife, listening from across the Ohio River in Louisville, Kentucky, would not question his absence from the air. After all, this was America's first manned Apollo flight.

Someone was required to sit at the microphone and fulfill the government requirement that the station be identified each hour. The program director chose me. I was a twenty-one-year-old college senior and had been hanging around the station for weeks to learn the ropes. For five years I had been knocking on the doors of stations in my hometown, begging for a chance. Station managers told me that the Louisville market was too big to hire beginners and that I should make my start in the smaller towns of Kentucky. I was just about to do that when the program director of this tiny blip of a station in Indiana allowed me to sit in his studio and observe.

Now he was away, succumbing to manly passion, and I had my opportunity. As the ABC anchor cued the station break, I flipped the switch and spoke the first words of my broadcast career: "This is WHEL, 1570, in New Albany, Indiana."

There were no fireworks in celebration and my debut escaped the notice of the local newspapers, but there's nothing bigger in a young man's life than realizing his dream. Never mind that I was working at the tackiest, most miserable little outpost in American broadcasting; I had crossed the threshold and joined the profession of Edward R. Murrow, Arthur Godfrey, and Red Barber.

Why wouldn't I be thrilled at joining the club? For nearly fifty years, broadcasters had informed and entertained Americans in ways that newspapers, magazines, theater, and motion pictures could not. They had made it possible for citizens to feel present at events occurring far away. Murrow's rooftop broadcasts during the London Blitz brought World War II into the living rooms of Manhattan apartments and Iowa farmhouses. Earlier, people short on hope during the Great Depression heard reassuring words from their president on the radio, and radio performers offered the only professional entertainment most Americans could afford. Baseball fans no longer had to gather at the local newspaper office to be relayed telegraph reports of the World Series. Graham McNamee in the twenties and Red Barber in the thirties magically transported fans in the bayous and the Rockies to the ballparks of New York, Chicago, and Detroit. Arthur Godfrey, on radio and then on television, brought a folksy personality to the airwaves and made his audience comfortable with the entertainers he introduced.

Broadcasting was run by people who, for the most part, believed they had a responsibility to listeners and viewers. The term *public service* was not uncommon in the early years of radio and TV. Broadcasting was a fabulously lucrative business, but money was not the only motivation. True, the programs were not always artful, challenging, and uplifting, but they were tasteful and responsible. Government told broadcasters they were to operate "in the public interest, convenience, and necessity," and most did.

Radio reinvented itself in the television age and began to rely on "narrowcasting," each station using a format designed to appeal to a distinctive demographic group. Television was now the mass-entertainment medium, with three commercial networks drawing tens of millions to their shows. Broadcasting drove pop culture. Radio and TV's *Ed Sullivan Show* had introduced us to Elvis and the Beatles—what next? TV had replaced newspapers as our primary source for news. Walter Cronkite was the most trusted man in America. I began my career at a crucial moment in the nation's history, and I believe it was also a critical time for communicators.

Broadcasting delivered the news of 1968, and most of the news that year was bad. We turned to radio and TV for escapist pleasure, and they betrayed us. They told us of young people dying in Vietnam and of other young people rebelling against authority. They told us about assassinations, riots in the cities, the Soviet crushing of the Prague Spring, and the chaos at the Democratic convention. Everyone seemed angry about something or somebody. Even the music was angry. In ancient times, rulers angered by news of a distant battle lost used to kill the messengers who brought them such bad news. In 1968, Americans began wondering if their messengers truly were their friends. Told by the scholar Marshall McLuhan that they should be more critical of broadcasters, they began using his terms for communicators. The trusted Walter Cronkite and his peers were now part of something vaguely sinister called "the media."

Running for election that year, Richard Nixon, who believed television had cost him the White House in 1960, showed how much he had learned in eight years. His campaign was run by advertising executives who were masters of the art of selling on TV. Nixon was a packaged product that year, sold to viewers who never saw him challenged in a forum that wasn't controlled by his handlers. This is standard practice in today's politics, but it began with the Nixon campaign of 1968. Once in office, Nixon's ideologues mounted a highly successful campaign to smear journalists, particularly TV journalists. A broadcaster's relationship with the audience would never be the same.

If the red-baiting anti-Semite from California didn't like journalists, it must be a club worth joining. Just days before Nixon's election, I reached for a microphone switch to speak to an audience for the first time. Astronauts were preparing to go to the moon, and I wanted to tell the world about it. Never mind that I was really telling only New Albany, Indiana, about it—it was a beginning. Finally I was doing what I had wanted to do from the time I was barely more than a toddler. I had waited long enough. I wanted in.

HOME

———

On the afternoon of May 16, 1947, my mother heard the Friday novena bell from our parish church as I was about to be born across the street at St. Joseph's Infirmary on Eastern Parkway in Louisville. The hospital was a fabulous period structure, its corridors lined with ancient radiators and cane-backed wooden wheelchairs. Sisters of Charity in their starched, white nursing habits scurried about the place, which I would come to know so well as a bronchial pneumonia patient just a few years later. My older brother had been born at St. Joseph's before my father went off to World War II. I was conceived as soon as the soldier returned, and my job was to complete the family in a gender-symmetrical fashion. They even had chosen my name: Mary Ann. I tried hard not to disappoint them after that.

I was named for a pirate. According to legend, Robert Edwards was an English naval officer who arrived in New York in the 1690s. For his service to the crown (relieving Spanish ships of their New World treasure), he allegedly was given a nice chunk of Lower Manhattan, property that now includes the Wall Street financial district. Edwards was said to have leased the land to a pair of churchwardens. When the lease expired, title to the property was supposed to revert to the descendants of Robert Edwards's brothers and sisters. For three hundred years, generations of people named Edwards have gone to court charging that

Trinity Church has cheated the family out of its multitrillion-dollar legacy. Lawyers over the many decades have made fortunes feeding the hopes of gullible Edwards heirs who have sought unearned fortune. Some of those lawyers have gone to prison. The scam continues today. My grandfather Edwards bought the story, but I doubt if he gave any money to lawyers. My dad always laughed at the matter and called it foolishness, but he hedged his bet and named me after the old salt who started all the fuss.

Mom and I were in the hospital for eight days, a routine stay in those days. The bill came to $71.30, of which Blue Cross paid $61.30. Ours was a family that kept receipts.

I was taken home to a tiny, two-bedroom house in a modest but pleasant working-class neighborhood of close-together houses, neat lawns, and used cars. There would be no car in our driveway for years. The neighbor on our right worked for the post office, and the neighbor on the left was a janitor. Other neighbors were plant workers, retirees, salesmen, and, curiously, one lawyer. Concord Drive was my home for twenty-two-and-a-half years.

We were not poor. By my definition, poor people go hungry some-times, but we always ate. *What* we ate was a bit strange, but we ate. I was in my twenties before I learned there were steaks and pork chops more than a quarter-inch thick with little or no fat on them. When I tasted my first prime rib in a restaurant, I felt decadent.

My parents had come of age in the Great Depression, and both knew hard times. My father, Joe Edwards, was the middle child of seven. As each child left for school, my grandmother stood at the door and in-spected their socks or stockings. If there were holes, she filled in the bare spots with black shoe polish. The children hated their father be-cause he was so hard on them, no doubt passing his own miserable childhood on to them. The product of Baptist farmers in Gravel Switch, Kentucky, my grandfather was still an infant when his mother died and he was placed in a Catholic orphanage in Bardstown. Following years of farm labor and a hitch in the army, he went to work for the Louis-ville and Nashville Railroad and wanted his three sons to follow him into the train yards. Two of them did, Tom becoming a machinist and

Pete a welder. Joe thought this sounded too much like hard work. He had white-collar ambitions and became the only one of the seven kids to graduate from high school.

Catholics once looked to the Democratic Party as their champion and solidly backed the Catholic Al Smith in the presidential race of 1928. My grandmother embraced FDR's New Deal and became a precinct worker for the Brennan Democratic machine, which ran Louisville in those days. She got her son Joe an interview with the local party bosses, who then found a patronage job for him at City Hall, sparing my father the hard labor of the rail yards. While taking college night-school courses in accounting, Joe rose through the ranks to become the city's chief accountant and deputy director of finance. The titles sound grand but the pay wasn't. When the Democrats were swept from office in 1961, I learned that my father, then in his peak earning years, had been making $6,700 a year. Even in the 1960s, that wasn't much on which to support a family of four.

My mother, born Loretta Fuchs, was the descendant of nineteenth-century immigrants—a baker from Austria, a dairyman from Switzerland, and tenant farmers from Germany. Loretta was just five years old in 1920 when her mother died of influenza. My grandmother sewed shirts for the soldiers at Camp Zachary Taylor and may have contracted the virus there. My mother was bounced around from one aunt to another, occasionally returning to her father's home, where her stepmother treated her the way stepmothers in old storybooks treated stepdaughters. Loretta also had a stepbrother who routinely beat her up. The emotional scars remained for the rest of her long life. When the abuse grew dangerous, a priest intervened and recommended refuge in a boarding school near Owensboro. An older, working sister paid the tuition. For the first time in her life, Loretta found some peace and happiness. But there was no money for a second year, and the fourteen-year-old had to return to the life of a child in the way, living with her grandmother for a time and, later, another aunt. On credit, she took a two-year business course in lieu of high school, then joined the working world as a bookkeeper.

One would think that Loretta's traumatic childhood would send her straight to the arms of the first man who offered some security; yet she told my father she couldn't marry him because she hadn't paid off her business course tuition. A man in love will sometimes act out of character—even Joe Edwards. In the only extravagant act of his life, Joe paid the last twenty dollars on her bill and figured he had removed the only obstacle to marriage. Loretta thought otherwise, but she married him anyway in 1939.

My parents were frugal people who stayed that way until they died. For them, the Great Depression never ended. In the 1950s, they finally bought a used car for a hundred dollars. Until then, they used public transportation. *Quality* was not a word in their vocabulary. The best brand was the cheapest—case closed. Every grocery item was checked against the receipt from the store, and errors of mere pennies in the store's favor meant another trip to the store for resolution. Our towels were premiums in detergent boxes. Glassware came from service station offers and jelly jars. Absolutely nothing was thrown away. I had to remain at the dinner table until I ate every last pasty lima bean and drank that awful syrup in which the canned peaches swam. To this day, I roll the toothpaste tube from the bottom and squeeze out the last bit. Soap bars are long past the bar stage when I'm still using them. Frugality is in my blood.

Air conditioning was out of the question—not even a window unit. No one else in the neighborhood had it either, and Louisville is notoriously humid. On hot summer nights we'd keep all the windows and doors open and hope for a breeze. That only made it easier to hear the traffic on I-65, the diesel horn from the Southern Railroad at the end of the block, and the roar from the stock-car speedway at the state fairgrounds just across the tracks. My sheet and pillowcase were soaked with sweat before the speedway crowd called it a night.

Childhood had its dark moments; there wasn't much sparing of the rod then in most working-class homes. And for years I never thanked God that it was Friday because the Friday routine was a problem. Following the dinner of bland tomato soup and a grilled cheese sandwich (meatless Fridays were not my parents' fault—that was the Church's doing) came the weekly flushing of the bowels, not my favorite legacy of my mother's German ancestry. The chalky taste of that laxative was not improved when the manufacturer brought out a flavored version of the product. It still bothers me that I had to bathe in my older brother's bathwater to save a few pennies on the monthly water bill. Would it have killed my brother to let me go first once in a while?

After graduating from Our Mother of Sorrows School in 1961, I entered St. Xavier High School, or St. X, as it's known locally. St. X was founded in 1864 by the Xaverian Brothers, a group of Belgians, Dutch, and other Europeans invited to Louisville in the 1850s by the local Catholic archbishop. Their job was to teach Catholic immigrant children, who were barred from the public schools by the nativist Know-Nothings who ran the city at the time.

St. X grew and prospered, becoming a sort of Notre Dame among high schools, offering a rigorous, challenging academic program and fielding championship athletic teams. Its goal is to turn out fine young Catholic men of strong character who are prepared for college. It graduates National Merit Scholars and future NCAA Division I athletes. Students are expected to meet certain standards in how they approach their studies and how they conduct themselves in and out of the classroom.

We were state football champions in my sophomore year. Two of my teammates made it to the NFL. The academic program was challenging but inspiring. St. X taught me I didn't need to be rich and gifted to succeed.

I graduated just in time for one of the biggest social revolutions in American history. The U.S. involvement in Vietnam escalated in 1965 as I registered for the draft, began a long string of full-time jobs, and started night school at the University of Louisville. The government restricted student draft deferments and decreed that they would last only four years. If I hoped to have a degree before I was drafted, I would have to take fifteen credit hours each semester and carry a full load each summer.

Young people protesting the war, the draft, and restrictions on civil rights fought a great many of those battles on college campuses. All kinds of experimentations with sex and drugs were incorporated into the politics, a stew stirred to an extraordinary sound track in an era bursting with artistic creativity. It was a fantastic time to be young, and I enjoyed it as much as my circumstances would allow.

A working-class boy without a college degree had few options be-sides infantry duty in Vietnam, so I regarded the degree as my life pre-server—and the work I did to pay for night school ultimately involved radio. *That* was the most important priority.

VOICE

Little boys want to be firefighters or athletes or rock stars. I wanted to be on the radio. The radio in our house was a handsome mahogany Zenith purchased by my parents when they married in 1939. Now decorating my living room, the Zenith Long Distance Radio remains a marvel to me. It's more than three-and-a-half feet high, more than two feet wide, and a foot and a half deep. It doubles as a piece of furniture, the perfect pedestal for flowers in a vase next to a framed portrait of Grandma. As a toddler, I ran my fingernails across the fabric covering the huge speaker at the base. Reaching high and to the left, I could touch the knobs and buttons (voice, normal, treble, alto, bass). To the right were the push buttons labeled with the call letters of stations that don't exist today. Frequencies were listed in clock-face fashion, shortwave stations forming the upper arc, the AM band on the lower arc. At "noon" on the clock face and out of my reach was the mysterious green light that peered at all in the room.

With a tall outside antenna, our radio could pick up foreign broadcasts, ships at sea, police calls, and ham operators, but we didn't bother with that. We listened to the network programs that had yet to make the switch to television. Soap operas were still on the radio; *Our Gal Sunday* and *The Romance of Helen Trent* were my grandmother's favorites. I remember hearing President Truman talk about the war in

Korea. Just before suppertime, a local priest would lead the rosary and Mom would insist that I pray along.

So many voices coming out of that box fascinated me. It didn't matter what the voices were saying; I longed for mine to join them. In time, I learned the formats of all the local stations and knew the schedules of all the announcers. At night, I heard other voices on stations in Chicago, Nashville, New Orleans, and Cincinnati, and I'd dream of seeing those places someday. Everything said on the radio had my attention in those days, not just the news. I would have been perfectly content to be the fellow who said, "You're listening to the music of . . ." or "Tune in tomorrow for another thrilling adventure of . . ." I just wanted to be one of the voices in the box.

At school, I learned to read aloud well. When a school play included a role for a narrator, I got the part, and I supplied my own prop. I fashioned a microphone by mounting the bald end of an old mop handle onto a wooden block base. At the metal end of the mop handle, I fastened an upturned soup can and painted the whole contraption silver. It was my first microphone.

At home, I read the newspaper aloud, sometimes in front of a mirror to see if I could maintain eye contact with a camera, like the newscasters on TV. I also worked on sounding like the men on radio and TV, and that meant losing my accent. No one told me to do that, but it was obvious that the people in broadcasting didn't sound like my Kentucky friends and neighbors. Except for country music disc jockeys and sportscasters such as Red Barber and Mel Allen, broadcasters sounded like Yankees. Losing the accent wasn't hard (it's all in the vowels), but I'm ambivalent about it now because accents are no longer much of a professional barrier. I feel I was forced to renounce some of my Southern heritage. Besides, not everyone appreciates the absence of colloquial speech. My high school football coach mocked my diction and vocabulary. He called me "the ambassador." This was intended to portray me as "delicate" and not the aggressive animal he thought a six-foot-four, 197-pound lineman should be. Instead, I chose to take it as a compliment.

While still in high school, I started visiting radio stations in the Louisville area. Most of the people I met had no time for a kid, but there were exceptions. Reed Yadon, then a newscaster for a tiny station downtown, was very encouraging. John Sharfenberger, known on the air as John Sharpe, let me use his studio to tape some newscasts, which he would critique. I think of them when a young person today asks me how to break in to the business. I know what it is to be a voice in waiting.

After graduating from high school, I spent three years working at a number of jobs that had nothing to do with radio. The money I earned paid for my college night-school classes, but these jobs weren't doing anything to establish a radio career. At twenty-one, I decided I wouldn't work at another job unless it was in radio. That's when I camped out at WHEL, watching, listening, asking questions—learning but not earning.

At this point, my father lost patience with me. I was still living in his house and eating his food but paying no room and board. He wanted me to sign on as a bagger at the local Winn-Dixie store, like many of the other guys in the neighborhood. I explained that my ambition was not to become the assistant produce manager of a supermarket but rather a broadcaster. He replied, "Yeah, and I wanted to play shortstop for the Yankees." He thought my dreams were unrealistic, not because I was a dolt but because people in our family had jobs, not careers. They worked in factories and rail yards, not at radio stations. That was true enough through his generation, but many of my cousins, the sons and daughters of those plant workers, went to college and are employed in more important work than radio.

Once I showed my father that I could make a living in radio, he was totally supportive. In the early 1980s, I was astonished when he agreed to a public radio station's request that he record a promo: "Hi. I'm Joe Edwards. I listen to *Morning Edition* for its in-depth news coverage, its timely commentary, and its interesting features. But mostly I listen to hear my son Bob."

This was a guy who, raising me during the McCarthy era, wanted no public profile for anyone in the family, lest something we said or did jeopardize his job at City Hall. We were to join nothing, sign nothing, and endorse nothing. If required to be at a public gathering, we were to sit in the back row and keep our mouths shut. Now he was on the radio telling strangers they should listen to his boy.

One day I told Dad about some accomplishment or milestone and he replied, "Yeah, and if you had listened to me, you wouldn't have amounted to anything." That was hyperbole, of course, but also typical of the cryptic speech of the World War II–era dads who were too macho to express emotion in a literal way. Translated, that sentence means, "Son, you were right and I was wrong. I'm proud of you and I love you."

His comment was an enormous leap for a guy who had so much pride. At that moment, he had completed all the obligations of fatherhood. He had played catch with me when I was a kid. He went to all my games even when he knew I'd never get off the bench. Now this. When he died in 1991, there were no unresolved issues.

WHEL

———

In my first three years of college, neither my academic nor my job performance was exemplary. I had to struggle for every C in class while inevitably getting fired from almost every job I had. After serving as a bank messenger and a trading-stamp-premium stock clerk (remember S&H Green Stamps?), I became a bookkeeper for an oil company, then an accounting clerk for a distillery (loved those discounts!), and finally a playground instructor for the county parks system. My favorite job was delivering flowers on Mother's Day. All the moms were thrilled to see me, and they all gave me tips.

But as my senior year began, I was determined, as I told my dad, that the anything-for-a-paycheck period was over. It was going to be radio or nothing. It could be argued that WHEL barely qualified as radio, but I was happy to be there.

New Albany, Indiana, is located at a bend of the Ohio River opposite the West End of Louisville, Kentucky. The southernmost part of Indiana offers the only relief from the state's relentless flatness. Indeed, New Albany's hills bear the colorful name of Floyd's Knobs. Honest. The village's principal architectural feature is a power plant on the riverbank, and its biggest tourist attraction is a steamboat museum in a fine old Victorian mansion. In 1968, the hot spot for entertainment was the piano bar of the Robert E. Lee Inn. Still, it was a charming town with a quaint quirk or two. Parking violators found a small envelope on their windshields. The miscreant was expected to put a quarter into the envelope and drop it into one of the collection boxes on the corner. Most of us did.

WHEL occupied the second floor of a music store at the bustling corner of Pearl and Main streets. A dark, forbidding-looking stairwell led to a landing lit by a bare lightbulb. Occasionally a wino found the stairs a convenient resting place. Women were reluctant to venture up the stairs alone, a major frustration for Mandy's Sample Shop, which shared the second floor with the radio station.

Walking on threadbare carpets that had never been cleaned, one entered the disaster area that comprised the studios and offices of WHEL. A visitor would not have known whether to request a song or place a bet. It looked as though a fire could break out at any moment. A newspaper writer described the furniture as being from "someone's early married period," an inventive phrase but much too generous. The walls had not been painted in my lifetime. As for the studio equipment, Marconi would have recognized every tube.

There was a heavy drape that might have once been yellow hiding the dirty window in the studio, but it couldn't muffle the sounds of the traffic outside. Listeners could hear tractor-trailer trucks on Pearl Street shifting for the turn onto Main. The Ohio River was sixty yards away, and one could hear the horns of towboats and even the steam whistle of the Belle of Louisville, an old paddle-wheeler owned by Jefferson County, Kentucky.

It did not look like "the home of the world's most beautiful music," which is how the station billed its format. It was "easy listening" music, just a step or two above the kind heard in dentists' offices. Music was played in blocks of three to five songs—instrumental, vocal, instrumental, group vocal, and, if there was time, a piano. So a listener might have heard Percy Faith, Nat King Cole, Mantovani, the Anita Kerr Singers, and then Eddie Haywood. A Sinatra tune would have been regarded as an up-tempo number. I donated some Basie, Ellington, and Earl Hines to the station library to liven things up a bit.

Saturdays sometimes were devoted to marathons featuring a single band—Glenn Miller or one of the Dorsey brothers. A listener once called disc jockey Phil Downs to complain that big-band songs such as

"American Patrol" and "Don't Sit under the Apple Tree" were too supportive of war. Phil replied, "I've got one here just for you, buddy," and cued up "Praise the Lord and Pass the Ammunition."

Commercials, if any, were clustered at each fifteen-minute interval. More often than not, the sale of our airtime did not result in a payment of cash to the station's treasury. There were lots of "trade-outs," an exchange of merchandise for an on-air plug. When a disc jockey said, "Embassy Supper Club time is 10:05," someone on the staff got to have dinner at a nice restaurant. Several times that lucky diner was me. So the commercials didn't bring an upgrade in salaries and equipment but rather new carpets and appliances at the homes of the general manager and the sales manager, both minor partners in the station's ownership. The principal owner lived far away in another city. I don't think I ever met him.

You'll recall that my first turn at the microphone allowed the program director to have a fling with a listener. That did not mean I was hired. I was still just a college student hanging out at the station. But my eventual hiring also had to do with the program director's sporting lifestyle. A few weeks after the guy's nooner with a fan, the police arrived at the station and arrested him for nonsupport of a previous wife or child. There was no one around to take his place except me. I went back on the air and this time on the staff, remaining there even after the boss got back from the pokey.

I was not the youngest member of the staff. Allen Brown was a seventeen-year-old high school senior. One day Allen saw me opening some record albums sent to us without regard for the type of music we played.

"What's that one, Bob?"

"I don't know. It's got an all-white sleeve with no lettering. Must be a demo or something."

"Let me see that."

Then Allen walked out the door with the Beatles white album. It *did* have some tiny lettering. It said "The Beatles" in white-on-white, easy to miss.

A broadcaster's first radio job is a joy, even if it's with a tiny outfit like WHEL. It didn't matter that the station had the horrible frequency of 1570 with just a thousand watts of power and a signal that couldn't carry across the river to my parents' radio unless the wind was blowing in the right direction. We had to sign off at sundown. That was fine in the summer, when we could stay on the air until 9:00 PM, but the 5:30 sign-off in December meant we were missing a good portion of the listeners' commute home in their cars. That, in turn, made us unattractive to advertisers.

The parsimony of the station was hilarious. The sales manager invited staff members to a Christmas party in the back room of a restaurant, and we were astonished at the ole boy's willingness to spend a buck or two on us. The party started at 7:00 PM. Finishing our coffee and dessert, we all looked forward to a few belts of holiday cheer. But at 9:00 PM, the sales manager wished us all a Merry Christmas and headed for the door, while the waiters started stacking our chairs. The sales manager had booked the room for only two hours.

The station could not afford a full-time engineer. Transmitter readings were taken by the announcer, using a remote unit in the studio. Once, during a test of the Emergency Broadcast System, I did the required drill of turning off the transmitter for five seconds. But when I tried to turn the transmitter back on, the remote unit couldn't do the job. The station was off the air. I had to run down to my car, drive out to the transmitter site, pop the rusted padlock on the old shed at the base of the station's tower, go inside to throw a switch, and retrace my route back to the studio. We were technically back on the air when I flipped the switch, but with no other announcer around, there was dead air until I returned. The elapsed downtime was about forty minutes, and nobody called to ask why we weren't on the air.

I did get a call one day from the manager of the other radio station in town. Yes, believe it or not, New Albany, Indiana, was a two-station burg. WNAS had 250 watts. Drugstores sell lightbulbs that run on 250 watts! The manager of this powerhouse had noticed the new announcer in town.

"Hey Bob, I've been listening to you. You sound great."

"Well, thank you very much. You're very kind."

"Say Bob, what are they payin' you over there?"

"Seventy-five dollars a week."

"Ohhh, I see. Well gee, we sure can't match that. But I wish you a lot of luck, young man." Click.

It was the first time that a competitor called to almost offer a job. That wouldn't happen again until 2004.

When I first joined the station, it was an ABC affiliate. We carried ABC News on the hour and the network's broadcast of Don McNeill's *Breakfast Club*, one of the last of the old-time, long-form entertainment programs still on radio. In the radio business, stations switch or drop their networks, but networks rarely drop a station. How bad was WHEL? We were so bad that ABC dropped us.

That left us without a news service, and in 1969 even the likes of WHEL felt compelled to fulfill its public-interest responsibilities. So the station installed a UPI wire machine, and we disc jockeys doubled as "newsmen" in the rip-and-read style, ripping news copy off the machine and reading it on the air, mistakes and all. Woodstock and the first moon landing were two of the big stories that summer. The noisy wire machine was kept in a storeroom, and there was no one around to maintain it. Often it would run out of paper, or the paper would jam, or the ribbon would break. That meant going on the air with the last readable news copy still available, even if it was several hours old. These problems were solved the day we couldn't pay the wire service bill and the machine was removed.

Dropped by ABC. Dropped by UPI. Now where would we get our news? Well, from the local newspapers, of course. Louisville's *Courier-Journal* was aware that a lot of local stations were stealing the paper's stories, but at least most of the stations managed to rewrite them. Our guys couldn't be bothered. Newspaper stories sound ridiculous when read aloud. Some of them begin with quotes. Others use quotes with the attribution at the end: "'I think it will be great for the city,' the mayor said today." We were still doing the news, even if you could hear us turning the pages on the air.

The events of the late sixties helped me focus on what I wanted to do in broadcasting. Spinning records was fun, but broadcasting the news to a national audience would be my way of being part of all the important developments taking place in the world. Vietnam, civil rights, moon landings, and all kinds of social upheaval were commanding public attention, and here I was in this rumor of a radio station playing Glen Gray and the Casa Loma Orchestra for the benefit of my mother and our other listener.

With encouragement and instruction from Bob Lewis, the senior member of the staff, I did my first reporting. I covered the news conference at which Actors Theater of Louisville announced that Jon Jory was its new director. Then I interviewed New Albany's Congressman Lee Hamilton. I was starting off in good company. Jory quickly turned ATL into one of the most important regional theaters in the country and remained in charge there for decades. Representative Hamilton served in Washington with great class and distinction for another thirty years and cochaired the 9/11 Commission.

In August of 1969, I finished my last college semester. After all those long nights, Saturday mornings, and summer semesters, I had met the government's deadline. Since there was no August commencement ceremony, I walked into the registrar's office whistling "Pomp and Circumstance" and strolled out with a bachelor's degree in commerce from the University of Louisville.

Washington wasted no time in notifying me that I was drafted. In November, I said good-bye to the people who had given me my start in broadcasting. The law required that veterans returning from service be given the jobs they held when they were drafted, but I knew I would never be returning to WHEL.

There is still a radio station on the 1570 frequency in New Albany, but WHEL is no more. A later owner turned it into a gospel station, and you can't be praising the Lord with HEL in your call letters.

ARMY

—————

I did my basic training at Fort Knox, Kentucky, and moved on to Fort Gordon, Georgia, where I married Joan Murphy. When I was sent to Asia—but not to where my fellow soldiers were dying.

When I arrived in Seoul in November 1970, there were more than seventy thousand American troops in South Korea, including two infantry divisions (one was sent home shortly thereafter). Wherever the United States stations its military, it tries to bolster morale and provide a little bit of home. That means entertainment, and entertainment includes broadcasting.

The American Forces Korea Network (AFKN) traced its proud history back to the Korean War. When I joined the staff, AFKN was operating a TV station that could be seen throughout South Korea. There were AM radio stations in eighteen locations, seven originating local programming, the others repeating the signal from the station in Seoul. There was also an automated FM station in Seoul. The TV station carried American news, sports, and entertainment programs on film without the commercials, plus live news and sports reports at 6:00 PM and 10:00 PM (just like back home) prepared by the AFKN news staff. The radio stations offered rock, country, and other music programs with AFKN staff disc jockeys (army and air force enlisted men). The stations had their pick of any American network's news and sports features, distributed to all military broadcasting outlets world-wide by the American Forces Radio and Television Service (AFRTS) in Washington. AFKN originated a lot of programs, interviews with visiting dignitaries, and remotes of USO shows, boxing matches, band concerts, news specials, and, of course, the annual visit by Bob Hope.

For me, AFKN offered a completely different environment. In Georgia, we were making training videos and devoting most of our energies to avoiding work. In Korea, we were doing actual broadcasting, as we'd been doing before we were drafted and hoped to be doing again after we were discharged. My new colleagues didn't like being in the military any better than I did, but they took professional pride in their work. One of them had been a DJ at a fifty-thousand-watt station; another had been a news writer at KNX, the CBS-owned station in Los Angeles; and a producer-director had won a local Emmy in Philadelphia. They wanted to keep their skills sharp. The mission was worthy too. We were informing and entertaining our fellow grunts, and if some officers also got informed and entertained, well that couldn't be helped. I also liked AFKN's priorities. If North Korean forces attacked, our job was to load up the remote truck and head south to safety. Now that's my kind of military unit!

Most of the U.S. Army installations in Seoul were located in Yongsan Compound, a nice chunk of real estate just a short taxi ride from downtown. AFKN occupied a sort of compound within the compound because it was isolated atop a hill. The studios and offices were in an ugly, cramped cinderblock building and a couple of new prefabricated structures. Living quarters were Quonset huts, individual "rooms" sectioned off by wallboard with curtains for doors. We worked, slept, and even partied on the hill because we had our own NCO Club. The 501 Club offered reasonably priced meals, a bar, and slot machines.

A few of the guys were content to never leave the hill, but most wanted to learn more about Korea and its people. AFKN encouraged this by broadcasting programs on Korean history and culture. It also sponsored an orphans' home for girls and threw them an annual Christmas party. Koreans knew all about AFKN. South Koreans watched and listened to our programs in hopes of learning enough English to get jobs at U.S. Army facilities. The airwaves carried our shows into North Korea too, and we were told that North Koreans could earn a reward if they captured one of us AFKN "propagandists." Unfortunately, the price on each of our heads was just twenty-five dollars. Then again, twenty-five dollars went a long way in those days before South Korea and other Pacific Rim economies experienced the "Asian Miracle" and outperformed the mighty Uncle Sam.

Living off-post was the best way to get to know about life in Seoul. Just in time for Joan's arrival, I was lucky to find an apartment two blocks from Yongsan. The landlord furnished a wardrobe because the rooms had no closets. I bought a Korean bed—a foldable foam mat three inches thick. Heat was provided by hot water pipes beneath the floor.

The crowded streets of our neighborhood were lined with vendors selling fish and black-market goods bought or stolen at the Yongsan Post Exchange. Women carried babies on their backs and containers of rice on their heads. Men pedaled bicycles with loads stacked up to ten feet high on platforms over the rear wheels. Other men carried these L-shaped frames strapped to their backs. I saw one man carrying twice his weight in bricks. Children playing jump rope wore the black, military-style school uniforms provided free by the government.

From every house came the pungent smell of kimchi, the fermented cabbage dish that formed the staple of a Korean's diet. Another aromatic treat was the "honey wagon," which employed a long, fat black hose to suction the privies (our building had plumbing). Men pushing carts of goods were fond of using the street gutter or the nearest wall for a urinal. Beggar boys and con artists accosted each American, perhaps offering to sell him a "skinny picture" of his "sister" for fifty won (about fifteen cents at that time). For slightly more, you could rent the "sister."

The taxi ride downtown was always an adventure. "Kimchi cabs" were tiny vehicles driven by men who were surly and adventurous. They believed the gas pedal should be pushed all the way to the floor whenever the cab was in motion. The brake pedal was not employed until the driver was a mere ten yards from his stopping point. The concept of lanes must be some silly Western notion. No one bothered to paint lines on the streets of Seoul.

Bargaining with clerks in downtown shops, I'd insist on paying no more than a fifth of the item's listed price. The clerk would agree and then giggle over how she had just snookered another American into paying twice as much as he should. I was drawn to Seoul's monuments, galleries, and museums. The gardens surrounding the pagodas and ancient palaces were a peaceful green refuge from the bustling hordes outside the gates.

Tearooms were the places for families to socialize and businessmen to make deals. I was not very adventurous in restaurants, where entrees looked like seaweed surrounding something dead that still had its eyes. The only safe dish for my Kentucky palate was bulgogi—beef with rice.

At a nightclub, I heard a Korean woman sing "Respect," selling the song as if she'd spent years in Aretha Franklin's church choir. She was Aretha's Seoul sister.

Back on the hill in Yongsan, I was learning about television, or at least TV the way it used to be. We were still broadcasting in black and white, using ancient TK-10 cameras. There was no videotape, just day-old film stories provided by ABC News. We made our own slides from photos and maps in newspapers. The slides could be seen full-screen, giving the news or sports reporter a break from having his face appear on camera (in case he had to scratch something). They could also be loaded into a rear-screen projector that produced the images on a screen behind the reporter.

I began doing sports but then moved to news, producing and anchoring *Newscope*, a summary of the week's news, and *Newsbeat Korea*, a summary of the week's news about Korea. Joan did the weather reports on the weekends, warning of ominous-sounding "Shanghai lows." She got into trouble once for saying the word "smog." Our host country assured her that South Korea had no smog, so she switched to "industrial haze."

We were free to say what we liked on the air, but we had to be careful what we said about Korea. Nominally a democracy, South Korea was ruled for decades by a succession of former generals. While I was stationed in Seoul, President Park Chung Hee was challenged by Kim Dae Jung, a young man of Kennedy-like charisma (he even had JFK's haircut). The election had the usual result, but Kim made a very strong showing and scared Park. Over the years, Kim was beaten, kidnapped, exiled in Japan, then imprisoned in Korea, and he was about to be executed when U.S. diplomats pleaded for his life. Korean politics underwent major changes. Park was killed in 1979 and his successors were jailed. In 1998, Kim Dae Jung became the president of South Korea.

Any incident involving the United States and the two Koreas was capable of renewing combat. In fact, China and North Korea are still officially at war with South Korea and the United Nations. South Korea did not sign the armistice of 1953, and there has never been a peace treaty. Over the years, the two sides have met near Panmunjom, a "peace village" in the so-called Demilitarized Zone, which I suspect is still riddled with mines and possibly missiles. Many meetings were tense and comic at the same time, with North Korea shouting at its adversaries, calling them "U.S. imperialist aggressors and their lackeys in Seoul." In one instance, the North Koreans decided their tabletop flag was not as large as the U.N. flag across the table. They brought a bigger flag to the next meeting. The U.N. representatives, amused to be playing flag war, placed their flag atop a book so that it stood taller.

I produced a story on Panmunjom and another on the transfer of a fighter wing from Japan to Kunsan, on South Korea's western coast. I traveled to Kunsan on a C-46, the same type of plane from which Eric Sevareid had to bail over Burma when he was covering World War II for CBS. At least Eric was issued a parachute—I saw none aboard. At Kunsan Air Base, the fighter planes landed, a band played, speeches were made, and the welcoming ceremonies concluded. When the Korean journalists had packed their gear and left the scene, so did the fighter planes. The crews headed back to Japan. The official transfer of the wing would occur at a later date. We had all just been part of a very expensive photo opportunity.

Dick Nelson, John Jessup, Frank Stanton, and Lloyd LaCuesta did most of the nightly news anchoring during my time at AFKN. One by one, they completed their tours of duty and went home. The next 6:00 PM anchor was me. I also produced a special report on the Pentagon Papers.

Working for the Rand Corporation, Daniel Ellsberg had access to massive amounts of secret papers that documented the whole history of U.S. involvement in Vietnam. Ellsberg believed the material should be made public and leaked it to newspapers. The Nixon administration moved to stop publication and the matter went to the Supreme Court, which ruled for the press. (We learned years later that another response to Ellsberg's leaks was the creation of Nixon's "plumbers," whose break-in at the Watergate Building would lead to Nixon's resignation.)

My special on the Pentagon Papers was strictly a cut-and-paste job. I wrote a simple narrative that laid out the story from the beginning. It wasn't fancy, but it was important. Many of my viewers had served in Vietnam, and others would be sent there in the next year or two. They deserved to know that this information was available and that the government paying our salaries was trying to keep the material out of the newspapers.

I wondered how the army would react to having me appear on camera in the uniform of the very army fighting the war and trying to prevent disclosure of its secret business. My paranoia increased when our civilian production chief, Ed Masters, told me the Eighth Army Command wanted to see my script. Taking a First Amendment stand is rather futile for a low-ranking enlisted man. A year earlier, some of my counterparts at the American Forces Vietnam Network (AFVN) had been muzzled and then reassigned to menial jobs. Ed assured me that the brass wouldn't change a word. They just wanted to make sure I wasn't going to say anything about Korea.

No grunt wanted the generals to know that he even existed. We wanted to melt into the background and avoid trouble so we could do our time and get back to civilian life just as quickly as possible. But it's hard not to attract attention when you're the evening TV news anchor. Walking across the post at Yongsan one day, I saw AFKN's secretary, Helen Hackman, running toward me and yelling to get my attention.

"Oh Bob, thank God, I found you in time. They've just had a big meeting at Eighth Army Command. They think your hair is too long and you're setting a bad example for all the troops. You've got to get yourself to the barbershop right away!"

So *that's* what generals do at meetings.

We did good work at AFKN, but we had our gaffes. One night, after wrapping up the newscast, we started the projector showing the next program, *Iron Horse*, an oater starring Dale Robertson. Then we crossed the driveway for dinner at the 501 Club. When we returned, we saw that the show had been running backward the whole time we were gone. Worse yet, no one had called to complain.

Someone did call to complain that we were running a program being narrated in Korean. We told him he was dead wrong; it was Japanese. We also promised to screen our films before we put them on the air.

Sportscasters Greg Lucas and Howie Halperin gave a blow-by-blow account of the Ali/Frazier fight for AFKN radio. They did this by watching the Korean network TV broadcast with the sound turned down. At the conclusion, Greg told his listeners about "a clear victory for Ali." Then he was horrified to see the referee raising the arm of a victorious Joe Frazier.

Finally, it was time to leave. I did my last newscast for Uncle Sam in August of 1971. The army was letting me out early so I could start graduate school in September. Joan left for Washington to find us a place to live.

Late one afternoon, I joined some three hundred others at Kimpo Air Base to board a Northwest Airlines charter for home. We checked our duffel bags, lined up on the tarmac, and waited. It is a cruel joke to tell three hundred young men that they are about to leave Asia and the army to head back home to civilian life and then have them wait. Our grunt paranoia set in.

We wondered if North Korea had invaded and we were going to have to stay in Korea for the duration of the war. It was more likely that someone in the group still owed a bill at the PX. We could see it wasn't mechanical trouble because no one was working on the plane. Maybe there was bad weather over the Sea of Japan.

After standing in line for about an hour and a half, we got our explanation when we saw a car flying a four-star flag. The top American general in Korea was putting his daughter on our flight and sending her home. After she boarded, the line finally moved. As we filed down the aisle past her seat, the general's daughter called out, "Hi Dave. Jim, how's it going? Hey Phil!" She seemed to know every guy in the Eighth Army except married me.

The plane stopped to refuel at an air base in Japan. While having a smoke in the coffee shop, I heard someone call my name. The speaker outranked me by a stripe, and I wondered if some lifer was going to put me on a cleanup detail during my final hours in uniform. As he got closer, I recognized Paul Ogden, a classmate from St. X. Paul was on his way home too, after driving tanks in Vietnam. I asked him how he reached the rank of sergeant first class. He said he was promoted each time a guy ahead of him in rank was killed. I didn't tell him how I had spent my time in the army.

As our plane took off, I looked out the window to my left and saw Mount Fuji bathed in bright moonlight. The pilot didn't bother to remark on the sight, and none of the rowdy passengers seemed to notice either. All they cared about was getting home and becoming civilians again. I thanked Mount Fuji for being there. It seemed a fitting farewell to Asia.

ED BLISS

Graduate school was not in my plans until I learned that enrolling in school for the fall term of 1971 could get me out of the army three months ahead of schedule. Education benefits under the GI Bill were not nearly as generous as those enjoyed by my father's generation, but at least they would pay for books and supplies.

Temple University offered me a graduate assistantship, but Temple was not my first choice because it had no broadcast journalism program. I wrote to Professor Edward Bliss at American University in Washington, D.C., and told him about my situation. He called me back a week or two later to say he'd match the deal. Washington appealed to me because it was a serious news town; the contacts I could make there would help me reach my goal of having a national audience. But the real attraction of the broadcast journalism program at AU was Ed Bliss.

While still in Korea, I had read the catalogs of the few colleges offering graduate journalism degrees in those pre-Watergate years. None of the schools had a faculty star to match Ed Bliss, who had spent twenty-five years at CBS News writing and editing—first for Edward R. Murrow and then for the first five years of *The CBS Evening News with Walter Cronkite.*

He had been where I wanted to go. Here was someone who could tell me how to get there. Once I got to know the man, his résumé became less remarkable than his many wonderful personal qualities.

Edward Bliss, Jr., was born in Fuzhou, China, in 1912. The son of an American medical missionary and an English teacher, Ed grew up in China and in Newburyport, Massachusetts. After graduating from Yale, he worked for newspapers in Ohio until signing on with CBS in 1943.

Ed eventually became night editor at CBS, and in 1955 he began writing Edward R. Murrow's nightly radio news summary. Ed worked for a time with Fred Friendly producing documentaries. Then in 1963, when *The CBS Evening News* expanded from fifteen minutes to half an hour, Walter Cronkite became the anchor and chose Ed to be the new program's first editor. The program opened with a two-shot of Cronkite and a balding man to his right. That was Ed, busy checking last-minute stories that might be inserted into Cronkite's prepared script.

Five years later, Ed told CBS legend Eric Sevareid that he'd like to teach journalism at a college. When Sevareid heard of an opening at American University, he told Ed, and a brilliant teaching career was under way.

Many successful journalists become teachers, but not always for the right reasons. Some are burned out and looking for a job they hope will be less stressful. Others reach a point where employers regard them as too old, too curmudgeonly, or too out of style. Journalists-turned-teachers often hope academia will let them coast on reputation and not require any of the heavy lifting of actual education. Ed Bliss was none of the above.

Ed was an enthusiastic educator who worked hard to prepare for classes. His lectures covered history, ethics, current affairs, legal considerations, fairness, good taste, news value, grammar, style, and the sounds of words when read aloud. Ed taught writing, the most important skill any journalist can have. He could not teach on-air skills, for he had never been on the air himself, and those skills are learned through experience. He could not teach someone to sound great if nature had not endowed the person for that. But he could teach one how to write, how to make oneself sound intelligent, and how to make the person who would be reading the writer's words sound intelligent. For that, he had no peer.

He taught us to have the highest respect for the audience—our readers, viewers, or listeners—the consumers of our work. He understood that we would be expected to please our bosses, but Ed told us that if our bosses failed the audience, then we should get new bosses.

A student teased Ed, accusing him of teaching just two courses: Edward R. Murrow I and Edward R. Murrow II. Ed didn't dispute that, for he believed Murrow's principles were still the best.

His uncompromised belief in Murrow nearly cost him his life. He was walking near Columbia University in New York and decided not to take the shortcut through the park to Morningside Heights because it might be dangerous. Then he recalled a line from Murrow's stirring broadcast about Senator Joseph McCarthy. Murrow had said, "We will not walk in fear, one of another." Ed decided he would not walk in fear, so he crossed into the park and got mugged. One thief took Ed's watch and wallet, while another held a knife at the throat of Murrow's disciple. Then the knife was pressed against Ed's stomach, the blade cutting through his shirt and the point pricking his abdomen. Ed believed he might be about to die and wondered what he could say that might cause the mugger to think this was a life worthy of being spared. Ed said, "I'm a teacher." I told Ed he was lucky the punk hadn't been terribly mistreated by a teacher. The story illustrates that Ed believed teaching to be a special calling worthy of respect.

Another tendency of the star-journalist-turned-faculty-celebrity is to favor suck-up graduate students who laugh at his jokes and swoon over his journalistic war stories. Not Ed, who would take the time to comfort a freshman who was homesick or upset about a boyfriend. I vowed I would never become a teacher unless I could have the same commitment as Ed.

Ed Bliss had attributes that would seem to be opposed to one another. He was a sweet, gentle, kind man we all wanted to adopt as our surrogate father. We were certain that movies, sunsets, and kittens made him cry. He was still crazy about his wife, Lois, after decades of marriage. We all knew for certain that he cared about us too. But it was his brutal honesty that proved it. He could not lie to us to make us feel better. If we didn't have the talent, he told us so. He could not do otherwise.

I thought I was a pretty good writer until I turned in my first news copy to Ed. When he returned it to me, it was a blur of blue, edited beyond recognition. Obviously, I had a lot to learn.

Ed told another student that she should change her major because she had no future in journalism. She burst into tears, but Ed's candor was exactly what she needed. She told this story years later when she was the congressional correspondent for United Press International and was thanking Ed for helping her succeed.

Our mentor taught us there was no such thing as a small mistake. If we mistook the foreign minister for the defense minister, confused the Balkans with the Baltics, or spelled *sheriff* with two *r*'s and one *f*, these were all grave, unacceptable errors.

He was equally unforgiving with the rest of the world. Ungrammatical advertising slogans infuriated him. "Winston tastes good like a cigarette should" offended him because the slogan employed *like* instead of *as*. It would have been enough to cause him to change brands if he had ever been a smoker.

I once tried to share with him a passage in a book. He took the book from my hands, pulled a pen from his shirt pocket, and edited the page.

"You can't mark that up, Ed. It's a library book."

"But it's wrong."

He once wrote a magazine article lamenting the demise of the hyphen in modifiers such as *hard-pressed* or *well-fed*. Former student Alex Chadwick was strolling with him when Ed reached for a pen and edited the temporary license plate on Alex's car, changing *thirty day tag* to *thirty-day tag*.

His manner of correcting us was all the more devastating for its lack of hostility. When I put two *t*'s on the end of Connecticut, Ed removed his glasses, looked me right in the eye, and sorrowfully said, "Oh Bob, I thought *you* knew better." This was like getting a poison dart to the heart. I had disappointed "Dad" and he was hurt. We felt horrible when he did this and would have preferred that he yell at us.

We loved him so much that our student evaluations were gushing compared to what we gave other worthy professors. When a member of the tenure committee held that Ed's lack of graduate degrees disqualified him for tenure, we formed a long line to testify on Ed's behalf.

It was obvious that Ed's professional associates also thought highly of him. We were treated to guest speakers such as veteran network journalists Dan Rather, Robert Goralski, Peter Hackes, Daniel Schorr,

Hal Walker, Bill Small, and Andy Rooney. None of them received a dime for addressing the class. They were there because Ed Bliss had invited them.

His network contacts paid off in other ways. We met Walter Cronkite at the CBS bureau in Washington and went to New York to watch the staffs of all three networks produce their evening news programs.

Students at other universities produced mock newscasts for practice, but ours were real. Each weekday, we produced two five-minute newscasts for WAMU-FM, the NPR station on campus heard by listeners from Baltimore to Richmond. As Ed's graduate assistant, my job was to produce those newscasts. I assigned some students to cover Washington news conferences and hearings on Capitol Hill. Others rewrote wire copy for stories to be read by the anchor. I edited their copy, and then Ed would edit my editing. We rotated the anchor assignment among all who felt comfortable speaking on the air. Students who had never worked professionally could list this experience on their résumés.

Ed's reputation also was a big plus when it came time for me to get a job. Sometime in the spring of 1972, he told me I should talk to Jim Snyder, who was then manager of WTOP-AM, the all-news CBS affiliate in Washington. Snyder took me on immediately as a freelance studio anchor. Snyder also had a solid reputation in broadcast journalism, and he would not have considered a twenty-four-year-old with my limited experience without the recommendation of Ed Bliss.

Alumni of the broadcast journalism program at AU have worked in every reputable newsroom. "Bliss grads," as we call ourselves, have served as network anchors, reporters, TV station managers, cable channel executives, foreign correspondents, and executive producers of evening TV news programs, both for networks and at major market stations. We've covered wars, natural disasters, and White House scandals. We've bagged all the big awards and spawned a legend. The Holly Hunter character in the movie *Broadcast News* was based on a Bliss grad. We're proud of our accomplishments, but we also know that Ed gave us the confidence to make something of ourselves.

In 1977, Ed was named Professor of the Year by the Society of Professional Journalists. The Association for Education in Journalism and

Mass Communication gave its most prestigious national award to Ed in 1984. The Radio-Television News Directors Association did likewise in 1993, giving him the RTNDA's Paul White Award, which is named for the man who ran CBS News when the network hired Ed in 1943. The Ed Bliss Newsroom was dedicated at the American University School of Communication in May 1996, with Charles Kuralt as master of ceremonies.

Ed Bliss retired from the AU faculty in 1977 but continued writing. Earlier in his career, he edited a collection of Murrow's broadcasts and coauthored a textbook on broadcast news writing. In retirement, he wrote *Now the News*, a history of broadcast journalism, which was published in 1991. *Beyond the Stone Arches*, a biography of his father, was published in 2001. *For Love of Lois* was a Valentine to Ed's wife, an Alzheimer's patient who died in the summer of 2000. By the time of its publication in 2003, Ed had also passed away at the age of ninety. At the time of his death, he was well into yet another manuscript about the glory days of CBS News.

Ed Bliss was my friend and mentor for thirty years. In my office, there is a photograph of Ed and me in 1972. He's very animated in this picture, clearly remonstrating with his young graduate assistant on the rightness or wrongness of something. Many years after my graduation, I learned that no one on the AU admissions committee wanted to accept me because of my undergraduate grades—no one except Ed. He said, "Look, this guy worked his way through college, and he's a veteran." The rest of the committee deferred to Ed and I was in. That decision totally changed my life. I think of Ed Bliss almost every day.

I helped endow a scholarship in Ed's name at American University's School of Communication. Each year I serve as a mentor to an AU graduate student because I know Ed would think that I should. My mentoring always begins with the story of Ed Bliss.

NETWORK

I received my master's degree in communication in August of 1972, after taking several courses at AU's School of International Service. A course on Southeast Asia provided historical perspective on the Vietnam War. The instructor was Kenneth Landon, a onetime missionary and diplomat whose specialty was Thailand. Landon had the distinction of being the author of the first Pentagon Paper, a memo he had written in 1945 recounting a conversation with Ho Chi Minh. Ho had asked Landon whether the United States was going to support Vietnamese independence following World War II or whether it was going to back France in reclaiming Vietnam as a French colony. It was an interesting document, but Landon's wife, Margaret, had done more lucrative writing. Her book, *Anna and the King of Siam*, became *The King and I*, one of the biggest hit musicals of all time.

It was an eventful summer for those of us at WTOP. The Watergate break-in occurred in June. The first accounts of the crime said the suspects were six Cubans, and that's how I remember telling the story to my listeners in the local news section of the broadcast: "Six Cubans were arrested by D.C. police last night at the Watergate office complex and charged with breaking in to the offices of the Democratic National Committee." I probably said no more than another sentence or two. A few weeks later, the *Washington Post* concluded it was more than a local story.

The political conventions that summer presented opportunities to earn some overtime. WTOP normally signed off at 1:00 AM, but we stayed on the air until we could wrap up our convention coverage. The Democratic convention ran so long that the party's nominee, George McGovern, delivered his acceptance speech at a ridiculous hour of the morning, or "prime time in Guam," as one wag put it. Nothing went right with the McGovern campaign. We would learn much later that a Nixon "dirty tricks" squad was sabotaging the opposition.

The summer ended with Hurricane Agnes, which, like many big storms, came ashore at Florida. Agnes, however, neither dissipated over land nor bounced out to sea. Agnes moved north and hugged the East Coast, occasionally moving inland and causing major havoc all the way to New England. Washington, D.C., rarely gets a hurricane, so the locals make no preparations. Agnes caused a lot of flooding in the area, and we on the night shift remained on the air until the morning shift arrived for their normal sign-on. I remember being in the studio and talking on-air with reporter Frank Herzog, who was driving along the Potomac.

"Remember Snake Island, Bob? Well there is no more Snake Island. It's completely under water."

All-news radio demanded much more preparation than that required for five-minute newscasts every hour. Each anchor had two hours to prepare one hour of material. That was hard enough to do for those working drive time, the commuting hours that constitute radio's prime time. Those of us working nights and weekends didn't have a lot of commercials, so we had to prepare more news copy to fill that time. When we finished an hour on the air, we'd spend the next two hours preparing another hour's worth of material.

The hour began with the network newscast from CBS. Then the local anchor billboarded the stories to come. Following a commercial, the anchor read local stories until thirteen minutes past the hour. Weather and another commercial came next, and then about four minutes of sports, beginning at fifteen past. Then there'd be a commercial, followed by a feature segment (a medical development, a consumer report, or maybe a commentary). This was also a good spot for installment three of whatever series an enterprising reporter had prepared for that week. The anchor gave the time and temperature every five to ten minutes. The back half of the hour reflected the front half, except there was no network newscast. The anchor read five minutes of national and international news instead.

The format gave the listener a sense of what was going on, but it lacked depth. Stories were not allowed to last three minutes or more for fear of tune-out by listeners who might be bored with that particular subject. It was assumed that a large segment of the audience was tuning in just to hear the headlines, so there was a bit of repetition of "the hour's top story." Of course, the station always had a big surge in listeners whenever there'd be an important, breaking story.

Probably owing to my lack of experience, I found the pace dizzying. There was too much to do—reading the news, weather, and sports copy—following the format to see that each segment started and ended on schedule while making certain that all the commercials ran. I was also doing my first live interviews. It's hard to conduct a live interview, which demands careful listening, while following a format and watching the clock, mentally doing the math to figure out how much time one has to complete the interview, do the commercial, and start the next segment on schedule. It was hard work, but I wanted to continue.

WTOP was a very good place to be in 1972. We were number two in the Arbitron ratings, doing news in a news town. The FM stations were still not competitive. I bought my first new car that year, and I recall that FM radio was still an expensive option, not considered standard equipment by Detroit. FM was so dormant that Post-Newsweek Stations, owners of WTOP, gave away an FM license that it wasn't using. The lucky recipient was Howard University, which continues to operate WHUR-FM as a thriving commercial station.

I was a freelancer, supposedly working part-time but getting enough hours in the spring and summer to be earning the salary of a full-time staff member. With vacation season over in the fall, my hours were fewer, so I asked Jim Snyder if he would hire me. Snyder said he had just one staff opening and he was giving it to the other freelancer, Jim Bohannon, who had more major market experience than I did. Well, there were no hard feelings because I liked Bohannon and thought he was a good choice.

Everything worked out fine, because I soon had a job doing two nightly newscasts for Mutual News. Not enough major market experience? I was going to be heard in every major market and all the minor markets too. At the age of twenty-five, I had achieved my goal of having a national network audience.

The Mutual Broadcasting System was founded in September 1934 by four big stations: WOR in New York, WGN in Chicago, WLW in Cincinnati, and WXYZ in Detroit. Its shows included *The Lone Ranger* and *The Shadow*. It was ambitious in covering sports (it was Red Barber's first network), and news photos of presidential speeches of the thirties and forties often show the MBS microphones at the podium.

But Mutual was always the poor relation among the networks, and it fell even further behind its rivals when it failed to follow CBS, NBC, and ABC into the television business. Ownership changed hands many times in the fifties and again in the sixties. The various owners included General Tire and Rubber, Armand Hammer, and 3M. MBS had at least one bankruptcy phase. In 1959, a federal indictment charged the company with taking money from the Dominican Republic's President Rafael Trujillo in return for favorable news coverage of the dictator and his country. When I joined Mutual on October 1, 1972, it boasted more than six hundred stations, but they were some of the sorriest stations on impossibly bad frequencies. It was odd that my first station, WHEL, was not an MBS station, because the two seemed made for each other. Mutual also counted as affiliates those stations that accepted money to run Mutual's commercials but wanted no part of Mutual's programs.

The network had tried to broaden its base by offering additional networks to serve minorities. I heard that the Spanish-language network failed because products used at the time by Puerto Ricans in New York apparently were unavailable to Cubans in Florida or Mexicans in the Southwest. Sponsors were wasting their money buying national spots for products available only regionally. By contrast, the Mutual Black Network was more successful and later was sold to Sheridan Broadcasting.

In 1972, Mutual's president was a big, blustery fellow who believed he could run a national network the same way he had run a small-market radio station in Florida. This included using some interesting sales practices, putting family members on the payroll, and trying to get rid of the union. His name was C. Edward Little. Little's wife, Totsie, ran the personnel department. Public relations was run by a guy named Bermuda Schwartz. I felt like I had walked into a Damon Runyon story.

The staff of the Mutual Black Network considered Little a redneck, particularly after he issued a memo saying they weren't sounding sufficiently "ethnic." Shock quickly turned to hilarity, with both black and white staff members employing our best Amos 'n' Andy impressions for newsroom communication ("Say, looka here, Sapphire!"). I don't believe the word *ebonics* was in use then. Most of the blacks on the staff had worked hard to lose any trace of an accent in their voices, believing that accents made people sound uneducated. One of the black newscasters was incensed, telling us that both his parents were doctors and he didn't want to sound like a fool. He said if he got another such memo he was going to tell Little, "I'll pick your cotton but I won't sing your songs."

The news staff at Mutual was represented by the American Federation of Television and Radio Artists (AFTRA), and the union contract was being renegotiated in 1973. Little hated unions and quickly determined which staff members were the most pro-union.

One of the big issues in the shop concerned our doing two newscasts for the price of one. We were to continue doing our regular newscasts, which were now sold as Mutual Comprehensive News. Then we were to do another version featuring more items but written shorter and read rapidly. This was Mutual Progressive News, intended to appeal to rock stations. In classic labor terms, this was a work step-up—more work for the same dollar. There were other issues, but this was the one I cared about.

As a publicity gimmick, an auto manufacturer announced it was naming an all-star football team composed of players at historically black colleges. This might have deserved some small mention on the Mutual Black Network but was of no great news value otherwise. Imagine our surprise when all newscasters were ordered to include this item in *every* newscast over the course of a day and a half. We were also ordered to mention the auto manufacturer's sponsorship of the team and were provided with tape of the company's executives commenting on the team while, of course, mentioning their company's products. This was not news; it was what we now call "product placement," and it did not belong in a newscast.

Every night I complained to my newsroom colleagues about such outrages, and we all traded jokes about Little. When I was told that I was among a dozen or so "union types" whose employment would end at the close of 1973, I figured we must have had an informer in our midst. A few months after my firing, a microphone was found in the ceiling above my desk. The microphone wire led to a tape recorder in a production room no one ever used. The FBI investigated, and while I don't think it was ever established that tapes of newsroom conversations were made, no one puts a microphone behind a ceiling panel to record the ambient humming of the heating ducts. The likely target of the bugging, if there was any, was our union shop steward, who occupied my desk during regular business hours. The mic would have picked up his comments by day and mine by night.

In another postscript to my Mutual experience, I took the matter of the black college all-star team to the National News Council. The council was a short-lived effort to get news organizations to act in accordance with certain ethical principles of good journalism. Its decisions were rendered in the form of opinions. There were no sanctions imposed on offenders and no penalty to pay except perhaps some embarrassment. I'll admit there was a revenge factor in my taking Mutual before the council, but I also still had a lot of the Ed Bliss–inspired idealism about journalism. I felt that we in the news business had a responsibility to the public. I believed listeners, viewers, and readers should have confidence in the truth of what reporters say. To that end, the offenders had to be reprimanded.

The National News Council heard my testimony and reviewed my documents, which included the memos ordering inclusion of the story with mention of the sponsor. Mutual declined to defend itself. The council presented me with its written decision totally in my favor. A copy was also sent to Mutual, which was given ten days in which to comment before the decision was made public. Mutual did not comment but instead sent its lawyers to the National News Council for a little chat. Then I received a second written decision by the council that completely reversed its previous decision. In the battle between corporate lawyers and an unemployed twenty-five-year-old, guess who won? The National News Council was not operating much longer. It probably died of its own fecklessness.

Shortly after I was fired, Little made a move that put some new life into Mutual. He hired a guy he knew from Florida to do a talk show from midnight until 5:30 AM. It was Ed Little who gave Larry King his first national audience.

Little never stopped trying to get rid of AFTRA. He even moved Mutual from Washington, D.C., across the river to Virginia, a so-called right-to-work state, where labor laws might be more in his favor. It didn't work. AFTRA even called a strike against Mutual, and I was proud to walk that picket line.

Little lasted nearly six years, until he had differing "management philosophies" with Mutual's owner, the prestigious Amway company. Mutual later was bought by Westwood One, which also bought NBC Radio. In the great consolidation of broadcast properties brought about by deregulation in the eighties and nineties, Westwood itself was bought by Westinghouse/CBS. Finally, in the spring of 1999, the Mutual Broadcasting System was allowed to die after nearly seventy years of operation.

NPR

I knew nothing about National Public Radio when I began working there, but I knew the reality of my situation. My severance money from Mutual was just about gone and I needed a job. I opened the phone book and called everything that had the word *radio* in its name. Just before I got to *radiology* and *radio repair*, I called NPR and talked to a producer named Rich Firestone. Rich said that the news director, Cleve Mathews, had a few projects in mind and I should talk to him. In fact, Cleve had just fired his newscaster and was just as much in need as I was. I made a tape for Cleve, and he told me to come back the next day and sit in with Bill Toohey, the New York reporter serving as temporary newscaster. Bill explained the format and had me do the 8:00 PM newscast. It was February 15, 1974, and I had a new job.

When radio began, all stations were noncommercial. They stayed that way in most countries and might have remained commercial-free in the United States if the government had resisted pressure from big business. Most of radio quickly became a new advertising medium, but some stations were licensed to schools, churches, libraries, labor unions, and other nonprofit groups. They were called educational stations until the 1960s. A few of the stations in the Midwest earned a following by providing information to farmers. In other places, such as my hometown, educational stations were the only source of classical music on radio. Lectures were common, and tapes were exchanged by stations in a sort of informal network.

The Public Broadcasting Act of 1967 was a part of President Lyndon Johnson's Great Society program. It was spawned by recommendations of the Carnegie Commission on the Future of Public Broadcasting. The Corporation for Public Broadcasting was created to sustain local stations and to grant funds for the production of programs. The Public Broadcasting Service would distribute TV programs nationally. There was a major flaw in all these plans. The Public Broadcasting Act made no mention of radio. Ultimately, noncommercial radio licensees successfully lobbied Washington to include them.

Public radio stations wanted something better than exchanging tapes. In 1970, they established National Public Radio as a production house for national programming and a nationwide distribution system. The first broadcast, in April 1971, was a session of the Senate Foreign Relations Committee's hearings on Vietnam.

On May 3, 1971, *All Things Considered* debuted as NPR's first regularly scheduled, daily program. That first broadcast included coverage of the massive May Day antiwar demonstrations taking place in Washington that week. Listeners heard reporter Jeff Kamen ask a police officer if driving his motorcycle into a group of demonstrators was a standard crowd-control technique. This was a new kind of radio produced by a new breed of broadcasters.

All Things Considered was the brainchild of Bill Siemering, a very bright and inventive man who loves radio and its service to communities. The mission statement Siemering wrote for NPR has a lot of wonderful things to say about the type of journalism the network would pursue. By the time I got to NPR, Siemering had been fired, and producer Jack Mitchell told me *ATC* was not meant to be a news program but rather "a magazine of the air." It gave listeners a mixture of aural experiences—the chatting of women at quilting bees, interviews with dulcimer makers, and commentary by storyteller John Henry Faulk, former New York Congressman Emanuel Celler, and early radio performer Goodman Ace. Mike Waters, one of the program's early hosts, produced a fantasy about God creating a sunset. Music and literature were important subjects to cover, and if the occasional piece of journalism crept into the mix, that was okay too. *All Things Considered* developed a loyal audience who loved the program's quirks and surprises. Critical reviews were favorable, and *ATC* won a Peabody Award in its first year.

I wish I could say that I walked through the door and immediately embraced this marvelous radio experiment. The truth is that I was horrified by the whole outfit. Public radio in those days had not fully emerged from its earlier "educational" incarnation. It had far more consultants than it had reporters. I didn't "get" NPR. I was still in my Murrow mode, a "serious journalist" too principled for my own good. Reporting the news was a religious calling and the radio airwaves a sort of church. I believed the news should be treated with the same reverence a priest gave to communion wafers. *Prig* might be the best word to describe me at that stage of my career. Now here I was, forced by necessity to be among people who were having fun with a radio program. How soon could I get out of here and return to broadcast journalism? Could I get away with leaving my NPR period off my résumé?

All Things Considered was a ninety-minute program heard live at 5:00 PM Eastern Time. I was hired to produce and read two newscasts, plus two more when a tape of the program was fed to stations at 8:00 PM. Resources were lacking, and I had to rely on freelancers and reporters at NPR member stations. In fact, the reporting staff was so small that I can still name everyone from memory: Linda Wertheimer, Ira Flatow, George Bauer, Barbara Newman, Bill Toohey, and Leo Lee. Sometimes I could get news spots from Josh Darsa, the producer of live-events coverage, or from Bob Zelnick and Judy Miller, freelancers who might as well have been on staff because they showed up every day.

I asked for an assistant and figured I'd be told to jump in the lake. Instead, I was allowed to do the hiring myself. That's how my fellow Bliss grad, David Molpus, joined NPR. David eventually brought Alex Chadwick and Jackie Judd to NPR. They were Bliss grads too. In addition to our American University group, there were other clusters of friends and associates recruited for NPR. One group knew each other when they all worked for Pacifica Radio. There was a New York contingent and another from Oregon. The pathetic NPR salaries were responsible for this hiring pattern. The network couldn't afford to pay experienced people what they were worth, so when jobs opened up, we contacted our pals. As a result, the NPR staff was young and not far removed from college. At twenty-six, I was one of the senior people.

Being young, we did young people's radio. There were no editors to tell us our work might be unbalanced or otherwise deficient. Production skills were lacking in the early years. One might hear a fantastic piece of radio followed by something so amateur that the reporter's mother would have hated it. It was frustrating to me that all this airtime available for quality journalism was being squandered on odes to vegetarianism and to people getting in touch with their feelings. Today I tell people that I was hired when NPR had no standards. It's a joke, but just barely a joke.

The flip side to the amateurism of youth was the boldness to experiment. This was one of the many virtues of NPR that I didn't appreciate at the time. We'd try anything at least once. There were few recriminations for failure—who else could they get to work for what they were paying? But when something daring actually worked—such as re-creating conversations with Richard Nixon—it was a great feeling.

President Nixon, under pressure to release the tapes of White House conversations, tried to placate his critics by releasing his own heavily edited transcripts of the tapes. This occurred on a weeknight. We had copies right away, but the general public in those pre-Internet days wouldn't see the transcripts until they were published in the Sunday newspapers. We thought the public shouldn't have to wait until the weekend to learn what was in this material. So we began a marathon broadcast in which we read the transcripts, each of us taking turns playing Nixon and his aides. It was impossible to determine what sort of inflection John Dean or H. R. Haldeman might have used speaking the words, so we were instructed to do all the reading in a flat tone without emotion, lest we "color" the words for the audience. Some of us tried to do that, but it was difficult because we too were hearing these conversations for the first time, and they were shocking. It was great fun hearing arts producer Fred Calland and legal affairs correspondent Nina Totenberg trying to give neutral readings of the conspiratorial rot being spoken by the highest officials of the land.

I was still plotting my exit strategy in August of 1974 when producer Jack Mitchell asked me to cohost *All Things Considered*. I neglected to tell Jack that I wasn't interested in a "magazine of the air." Instead, I took the job.

Over at the White House, Nixon was changing jobs too. The Watergate story had followed me through three different employers. I had done it as a local story for WTOP when "six Cubans" were arrested at the Watergate. After broadcasting the bulletins telling of "the Saturday night massacre," I wouldn't have been surprised to see tanks as I emerged from the basement studio at Mutual, then located just one block north of the White House. Now I was at NPR doing the talk-up to the story's final chapter—Nixon's resignation speech.

Vietnam, the other huge story of that time, was also reaching a climax. The last day of the war was the first day I opened my eyes to the possibilities for NPR.

North Vietnam's army rolled into Saigon in April 1975, dramatically ending a long war that killed soldiers from four continents. America's former allies and their dependents crammed into the last helicopters to leave from the roof of the U.S. embassy. Saigon was renamed Ho Chi Minh City. No longer were there a North Vietnam and a South Vietnam, just Vietnam.

One did not have to serve in Vietnam to be affected by the war. Vietnam was the reason I served in the army. Vietnam determined that I would go to college. It dictated which college I attended, the hours I attended, and the courses I took. It was responsible for my pre-army job history and the fact that I was married. Because of Vietnam, I met Ed Bliss, got a master's degree, and a recommendation for a good job at WTOP. Vietnam was the reason I was in Washington, and I probably never would have worked at NPR if I hadn't been living in Washington. From 1965 through 1975, Vietnam had touched every part of my life.

The place for me to be on that last day of the war was in front of a microphone telling the story to my listeners. Unfortunately, I was not at NPR in Washington; I was in the CBS newsroom in New York taking a writing test. I was acting on what I thought was still my dream, to broadcast the news for the place that Murrow and Cronkite had built. But during my brief visit, that dream died and a new one took its place.

The CBS newsroom was a chaotic scene that day as the staff coped with assembling the network's coverage. It would be the best reporting that anyone would hear on an American commercial radio network. That, however, was the problem. The coverage of this very important story was being tailored to satisfy the demands of commercial radio stations. Most of those stations cared little about the fall of Saigon. On commercial radio, the war had ended when the last U.S. combat troops left Vietnam three years earlier. Commercial radio stations wanted headlines and sound bites crammed into a five-minute block. Then it was back to whatever format won them a good Arbitron rating. You got the historical perspective? Fine, just give it to me in less than sixty seconds.

The people around me that day were doing a decent job, but I knew my colleagues back at NPR in Washington were doing a better one. They'd be lining up all the old diplomats and generals. There would be reaction from Vietnam vets, war protesters, and Vietnamese ex-iles. Scholars and pundits would share their views. Someone probably would produce a sound montage covering ten years of speeches, anti-war chants, and music. Once more our listeners would hear "Hey, hey LBJ," "four dead in Ohio," and "peace with honor." It would be a thorough, in-depth marking of an important moment in history. NPR stations and their listeners would expect nothing less.

I felt like something of a traitor and I was ashamed. Though NPR could be downright daffy at times, it was a place with its priorities in order. It rose to the occasion on important stories. It had no advertisers to satisfy and served its listeners instead. It did not exist to sell products. It produced quality programs because it could.

Back where I belonged, on *All Things Considered*, I approached my job with a new attitude, and I was rewarded by seeing improvement all around. I even warmed up to feature reporting, and I recall a story on the popularity of home birth (very big in the seventies) that contained a fabulous bit of tape. The midwife was having the mother give those final big pushes when the telephone rang. The mother's five-year-old entered the room and said, "Mom, it's for you."

The staff was upgraded too. Executive producer Jim Russell had made a disastrous hiring mistake and swore to all of us that he would never again hire anyone who was not a senior producer or senior reporter at an NPR member station. Sure enough, the next production assistant he hired was Noah Adams, a producer-reporter from our station in Lexington, Kentucky.

NPR was maturing and so was I. In 1975, my marriage ended, and I lived alone for the first time in my life.

SUSAN

———

Professional marriages are even more difficult than the romantic variety, and the divorce rate is much higher. Mine survived a tepid honeymoon to blossom into a rewarding on-air partnership and enduring friendship.

Susan Stamberg was a writer and tape editor for *All Things Considered* when the program debuted in 1971. Women didn't anchor broadcasts in those days. They worked behind the scenes and made occasional contributions on the air. But when Susan filled in as cohost one day, the phones lit up with calls from appreciative listeners. She was a sensation—refreshing, intelligent, engaging, and honest. She wasn't just warm and personable; she was way out there, reacting to a guest's humor with an infectious laugh that defied description. Men were charmed by her. Women took her to be their champion. By sheer force of personality, Susan took over the broadcast, becoming the first woman to anchor a nightly national news program.

Susan was great radio, the perfect performer for the aural medium that appeals to the ear and the mind. You'd think that a guy like me who'd spent his life loving radio would recognize a natural-born radio personality and be thrilled to work with her. Not Mr. Prig. I was in shock, wondering what in the name of Edward R. Murrow and all that is holy is this woman doing on a *news* program.

There was more to it, of course, including jealousy. Susan had been carrying the network on her back and was treated accordingly. We were supposed to be a team, cohosts, and yet all the attention was going to Susan. Later I learned that the policy of NPR's publicity department at the time was to throw everything behind Susan. Not only was she marketable, but the suits thought I wouldn't be at NPR for very long. Given that I was in the CBS newsroom on the most important news day of 1975, that was a reasonable assumption.

Susan made more money than I, though not nearly what she was worth. She also got whatever interviews she wanted, including some that I wanted. We tried interviewing one or two guests jointly, but without success. I persisted in trying to get John Erlichman to admit that his participation in the Watergate conspiracy was not a good thing while Susan steered Erlichman down a more productive path.

Her workday was shorter too. *All Things Considered* was broadcast from 5:00 PM until 6:30 PM and repeated on tape at 8:00 PM. Susan routinely went home at 5:30 PM to be with her family. To facilitate her early exit, the middle half-hour of the program was prerecorded in the midafternoon. Then Susan would read the introductions to a couple of stories that were scheduled to run in the final half-hour. At 5:30, Susan would go home and I would remain in the studio doing my half of the program. If there was breaking news or the need to do a live interview, it was my responsibility. I also had to do the updating for the 8:00 PM feed, though on special occasions, such as the night Nixon resigned, Susan would return.

Professional jealousies likely would have doomed our partnership had not other factors come to the rescue. Success offers a certain remedial balm for one's troubles. Susan and I were successful. Whatever tensions were in the air, we kept them *off* the air. Listeners heard a couple of people they liked and kept tuning in. The audience was growing.

When I made my peace with NPR, I also made my peace with Susan. She was my partner, and the professional thing to do was to make it work. She was also winning me over. In fact, I discovered that I'd been unconsciously learning from her. Susan changed the very way I sound on the air, talking *with* listeners and not *at* them. In a long-form program such as *All Things Considered,* the interviewer's questions are just as important as the guest's answers. I learned from Susan how to ask interesting questions—turning an interrogation into a conversation. The most important thing I learned from her was how to extend my personality on the air. One cannot host a program by sounding like a newscaster reading copy. A host has to sound like charming company, someone you want in your car pool or to have over for drinks on the patio. Susan helped me sound that way.

I admired the way Susan handled adversity. Every radio program gets at least a bit of hate mail, but at *All Things Considered,* the ugly letters took the form of anti-Semitic screeds directed at Susan. Garbage like that really upset me. It undoubtedly upset Susan even more, but she never let it rattle her. She never stopped being Susan.

Conceding all of Susan's interests to Susan, I carved out my own niche, principally by doing stories on Appalachia. This proved to be very rewarding because I had the field to myself. Appalachia usually gets press when there's a miners' strike or a mine disaster. I found the region as rich as Ireland in the number of superb storytellers. There's great radio to be mined in the mountains.

Susan and I learned to make use of our differences—artsy, Jewish female from New York meets newsy Catholic male from Kentucky. Each of us could usually fill in the blanks for the other. We played to one another's strengths and covered one another's weaknesses. I would feed her straight lines knowing she'd "sell" the punch line. She returned the favor by laughing at my jokes.

The cohosts were now living up to their titles. I produced a half-hour show about elevators and found a part for Susan. I had her ride the elevators in NPR's building and talk with passengers about elevator etiquette—no touching, no whistling; keep your eyes on the numbers or stare at your shoes.

If cohosts merely alternate reading scripts, you have two voices on the program, but you don't have two personalities sharing the program. There's a much better sound to the program when cohosts are involved in the same bit. Susan wrote the scripts containing excerpts from letters written by our listeners. Reading listener mail on the air was great fun when I adopted the listener's voice. If the listener was angry about something we'd done, I tried to vocalize the listener's anger. Susan was great about parceling out some zingers for me to read while retaining a few for herself.

Another shared script might be based on some research done by our trusty NPR librarian, Rob Robinson. For example, President Jimmy Carter's early 1977 proposal for a fifty-dollar tax rebate was too good to resist. We had Rob compose a list of what fifty dollars would buy. The options included 150 McDonald's hamburgers, 28 six-packs of Pabst Blue Ribbon, one share of GE stock, and a 71-mile metered taxi ride from midtown Manhattan to Ellisdale, New Jersey. It would be an interesting inflation study to see how many hamburgers fifty dollars would buy today. My favorite item on the list was 385 thirteen-cent stamps. Yes, we used thirteen-cent stamps in 1977. Carter soon withdrew his proposal for the rebate. I wonder if our bit of fun had anything to do with his decision.

Listeners got in on the act too. We had what we facetiously called contests. They weren't really contests because we never declared a winner, and the only prize was getting one's entry read on the air. We asked listeners to send us pieces of good advice they'd received over the years. We also requested suggestions as to what China's leader Deng Xiaoping should see when he made his historic visit to America (Filene's basement in Boston; a hot tub in Marin County, California; Billy Carter's gas station in Georgia). During the bicentennial in 1976, listeners helped us create a time capsule for the tercentennial in 2076. When scientists decided to add a "leap second" to correct the official clocks, we asked listeners what they'd do with their extra second of time. One said she'd have second thoughts.

This was interactivity in the days before online chat rooms and before the proliferation of so many radio call-in shows as cheap substitutes for more creative programming. Many of the ideas for listener participation came from Susan herself. She was always looking for ways to involve the listener and offer relief from the drone of stories on inflation and partisan politics. Susan loved her audience. Five minutes before the program, she would powder her nose and apply lipstick to be ready to greet the listener who could only see her in the mind's eye.

Working with Susan spoiled me for any future partners. I learned that working with pros helped me become a pro. Conversely, working with slugs won't make one stand out from the rest; it makes one resemble the other slugs. If I ever again have to share a program, I'll know how to do it, but I won't want to do it unless I can have the sort of relationship I had with Susan.

The partnership lasted five years, ending when I left *All Things Considered* to start *Morning Edition*. The friendship endures. I'm so sorry that the poor woman had to put up with a cohost who was still growing up. She was much more patient than I deserved, and she's classy enough not to remind me of it very often.

Today Susan Stamberg is NPR's special correspondent, a title I hate. What are the other correspondents—chopped liver? On the other hand, her stories of artists and the creative process are usually the most interesting pieces in the program. It's impossible to hear her and not pay attention. You'll usually learn something you didn't know, and you'll be entertained in the process. That's why the special correspondent is special.

ALL THINGS CONSIDERED

———

By the mid-1970s, NPR had developed an excellent reputation with a small but loyal and very appreciative audience. We had respect within the industry too, as other networks began luring away our reporters. That was not hard to do, given the salary disparity between commercial and public broadcasting. Something had to be done.

We tried forming an NPR Employees Association as a means of taking our concerns about salaries and other grievances to management. NPR insulted us with paternalism, making us feel that merely consenting to a meeting was doing us a favor. We needed some muscle, so we organized.

The American Federation of Television and Radio Artists (AFTRA) informed NPR that enough of us had signed up to warrant an election. The NPR management of that era didn't know the Wagner Act from Taft-Hartley, so it got some muscle in the form of one of those law firms that fights workers. The firm had management issue a series of bulletins telling us how good we had it and how a union would make our lives miserable. We were told that unions were anathema to our quaint, nonprofit, public radio "culture." We were told that a union would demand restrictive work rules that would result in our no longer being allowed to edit our own audiotapes. What they said about salaries at commercial stations and networks was laughable. At a time when Barbara Walters was becoming the first news employee to make a million dollars a year, NPR was telling its employees that our salaries were competitive with commercial broadcasting. In fact, I was cohosting the network's premier program for $17,000, and our best production assistant was making $6,900 a year.

Another ploy by management showed just how much it was out of touch with its staff. NPR insisted that the bargaining unit be expanded to include employees who produced arts programs. This was an effort to dilute the voting strength of the greedy, Philistine news-types by adding sensitive arts-types too noble to want to be paid more for their work. We did not contest the move because, in the event of a strike, NPR would have those very people producing *All Things Considered* in our absence. Better to get them into our unit and take them with us if we walked. To management's astonishment, production workers (news and arts alike) voted for AFTRA. Management was able to get only two votes.

We had a union but no contract. That took much longer and involved another propaganda campaign in which management tried to drive a wedge between union and nonunion employees. The rancor continued until 1977, when public radio stations decided to upgrade the management of NPR. I suspect the stations acted for reasons other than labor troubles, but their action had immediate positive results.

Frank Mankiewicz was the new NPR president, and one of his first decisions was to sign a contract with AFTRA. It was a brilliant gesture that immediately got us on his side. Frank had been a journalist and identified with us. He respected our work and understood our problems. He hung out with us and loved to swap stories with NPR reporters. He had been our fan as a listener, and now he was our leader.

Frank was perfect for NPR at that time. He was a public relations dream with many contacts in numerous fields. The son of screenwriter Herman Mankiewicz, who won an Oscar for *Citizen Kane*, and the nephew of legendary producer Joseph Mankiewicz, Frank grew up in Hollywood and graduated from UCLA. Bored with practicing law, he joined the Kennedy administration as director of the Peace Corps in Latin America. As Robert Kennedy's press secretary, it was Frank Mankiewicz who announced to the world that the senator had died.

He wrote books, anchored a TV news program, and then he codirected George McGovern's presidential campaign in 1972.

Newspaper reporters loved him because he was great copy. It wasn't just that he knew the important people in show business, journalism, and politics; it was how he told the stories. He was (and is) a superb raconteur, a master schmoozer. Journalists didn't interview Frank; they took notes. Once he became president of NPR, Frank continued to spin yarns about movie moguls, the Kennedys, and the boys on the bus, but his main message concerned a fledgling radio outfit that was providing more journalistic context than the major networks with all their resources. Newspaper writers might have heard something about Susan Stamberg's being the first woman to anchor an evening news program, but that didn't send them to their typewriters in great numbers. Now they were hearing about Susan and me from a guy with whom they could drink their lunch while stealing a few of his jokes.

Thanks to Frank, there were stories about us in *Time, Newsweek, Saturday Review, People*, the *Wall Street Journal*, the Associated Press, and most major dailies. At no cost to NPR, Frank was getting the kinds of results one normally gets only with an expensive ad campaign. We no longer had just a cult audience; we were starting to reach the masses.

It is impossible to calculate the positive effect this had on morale. We were the plucky underdog taking on the big papers and the network giants. We paid fifteen grand tops to a twenty-five-year-old reporter who would put together eight minutes telling you not just who said what but also why it was said and, more important, what was left unsaid and why. The network competitor would breeze over the highlights in a minute and ten seconds if he was lucky enough to get his story on the air at all, but he'd look great telling it.

The superficiality of TV journalism should have been obvious, but Americans respect money. Popular opinion says, "If you guys are so great, why aren't you working for the TV networks paying the big bucks?" This is a question we often asked ourselves, and several dozen answered it by leaving NPR when mortgages and tuition bills needed attention. Those of us who remained behind tried in vain to explain that the nonprofit nature of NPR made us a more credible news organization and, in a just world, reporters would not be compensated on the basis of how their hair looked on camera. It was a lonely argument until Frank Mankiewicz got the attention of writers who spread the word that NPR was reporting the news more thoroughly than other broadcasters.

The commercial networks' evening newscasts were barely more than headline services. Each broadcast was thirty minutes, including commercials. *All Things Considered* had ninety minutes without commercials. That gave us lots of time to provide historical context and explain complicated policy. We could itemize the bargaining that produced a bill, list the winners and losers, and explain what impact a new law might have on a given community. Congressional coverage by Linda Wertheimer and Cokie Roberts was so detailed and fair that both women became favorites of many on Capitol Hill. Congress also liked NPR because we were just about the only broadcast journalists covering congressional hearings in those days before C-SPAN. Linda anchored coverage of the Panama Canal debate, the first broadcasts ever from the Senate chamber.

Our strength was explaining the news, not scoring scoops, though Nina Totenberg had more than her share of exclusive stories. Jealous competitors on the legal-affairs beat told their editors that Nina couldn't be getting those stories on her own ability; she had to be sleeping with the justices on the Supreme Court. Being outreported doesn't bring out the best in journalists.

Scott Simon and Robert Krulwich were among the new voices adding to the rich variety on *All Things Considered*. Scott's narrative style made each of his stories a minidrama. He opened our Chicago bureau in time to report on the last days of the old Daley machine. Robert became the most entertaining journalist in broadcasting, not easily done when the subjects are inflation, monetary policy, and wage and price controls. If I tell you that his stories included the voices of radio "mice" and an economic policy debate set to opera, then you understand the limitations of the printed page when compared to radio.

Some of the stories about us declared that we were a throwback to the early days of radio. Perhaps the writers meant to say we were reviving the spirit of early radio. They could not have been describing our program. No one in the early days of radio was doing anything like what we were doing on *All Things Considered*. We were doing old-fashioned reporting in exciting new ways, and we were having great fun doing it.

At that time, NPR was located at 2025 M Street in northwest Washington. Across the street at 2020 was the CBS Washington bureau, the workplace of Dan Rather, Marvin Kalb, Bernard Kalb, Bob Schieffer, and so much of the finest talent ever in broadcast journalism. That's why Roger Mudd titled his memoir *The Place to Be*. Looking out my window, I'd see Eric Sevareid, looking like some stoic Norse god, trying without success to hail a taxi. Was he known to the cabbies as a lousy tipper?

I used to wonder if those CBS people were aware of their public radio neighbors, the scruffy-looking characters in jeans and flannel shirts who rubbed elbows with their tailored suits at various M Street shops. Buying a shirt at Christopher Kim's, I learned the proprietor was conscious of TV fashion. "Must have red tie," he said. "All CBS have red tie." I reminded him that I worked in radio and didn't need a necktie, but he insisted. I still have that red tie.

One of our producers, Clem Taylor, crossed to the other side to work for CBS. When we met on the street one day, Clem introduced me to Jed Duvall, then a junior reporter at CBS. Duvall said he knew all about NPR and envied the ability of our reporters to shape a story and not have it "lawyered" through so many filters that it no longer resembled what the reporter had written. I said I was sure he didn't envy us when he was in line at the bank. True, he conceded, but he called TV pay "the velvet trap," by which he meant there were numerous concessions he had to make to earn all that dough. He wasn't telling me anything I didn't already know, but it was nice to be reminded once in a while.

I was eating lunch at a sidewalk café one day in the seventies, and Daniel Schorr was at the next table. He must have just read a story about the merits of vitamin C, for his salad consisted of an entire plate of cherry tomatoes. Watching Dan eat his tomatoes, I recalled that Murrow himself persuaded Dan to join CBS News. Posted to Moscow, Dan managed to get Soviet premier Nikita Khrushchev to appear on *Face the Nation*. Dan was also in Berlin on the day East Germany started building the wall. His Watergate reports so enraged the White House that he was placed on Richard Nixon's enemies list. Later, his leak of a congressional report on the CIA would end his CBS career and nearly land him in prison. In his nineties (a good argument for the cherry tomato diet), Dan was still calling his sources and analyzing the major issues of the day. He no longer reported for CBS, which considered him a pain in the butt, and not for CNN, where he was a prominent early presence until Ted Turner decided he didn't want any commentators. Dan finally worked for NPR, where he had plenty of airtime to provide historical context and present a fully developed essay. Commercial broadcasting no longer had room for people like Dan Schorr, but public radio did. When Dan died in 2010, he was the last person hired by Edward R. Murrow to still be involved in daily journalism.

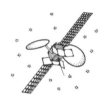

SHARON

The late seventies were good to me. I lived in Washington's Dupont Circle neighborhood, a lively area of bookstores, galleries, nightclubs, restaurants, and interesting shops, within walking distance of the Mall, Georgetown, and NPR. It was the perfect place and time to be young and single. Some of my relationships were not long-lived, however. They often would end when women determined I had no interest in marriage and family. I resolved that I would set things straight right at the beginning with the next woman I dated.

Sharon Kelly was an adorable, blue-eyed blonde who worked at NPR. I took her to lunch and discovered she was also bright, well-read, an English major, and very funny. As a bonus, she even laughed at my jokes. It would be a while before she learned that I stole all my material from professional comics. Over steak and fries, I explained that I just wanted to show her a good time and not get caught up in any serious commitment. I believe the term I used was *no strings*. "Sounds good to me," she replied, pointing out that she was on the rebound from a failed marriage and not ready for an encore.

This conversation took place in the spring of 1978. By June, I was no longer dating anyone else. By July, I was hardly ever in my own apartment. In October, we rented a house together. We were married the following May, and three months later we were expecting a baby. So much for no strings.

I couldn't help myself. Everything seemed better with Sharon than it had been with anyone else. She was the one. I didn't want to take a chance that this mutual freedom notion could be sustained, so I married her before she could get a better offer. Sharon changed my feelings about marriage, but it was a third party who changed my feelings about family. Sharon had a son.

Brean Campbell was a handsome, charming, bright little guy with a big smile and a wonderful disposition. Good thing he had all those wonderful qualities, because my dates with his mom evolved into outings for the three of us as a sort of de facto family. On my way to getting it on with this cute blonde woman, I found myself tying shoelaces for her three-year-old, taking him to the men's room at restaurants, applying the Band-Aids, and having him fall asleep on my lap in the car. I was in way over my head.

The relationship between Sharon and Brean astonished me. I had never seen a mother so devoted to her son. She read to him for hours. She stayed by his side when he was frightened or otherwise needed comforting. On weekends, they had great adventures—seeing a show, visiting the petting zoo, blowing bubbles in the park, and acting as extras in the movie *Hair*. Sharon spared nothing in trying to stimulate Brean's young mind, but it was the commitment to his emotional needs that so touched me. This was some serious nurturing.

So now I was about to marry the perfect mother for children I didn't know I wanted until I had forged a bond with Brean. Naturally he was the best man at our wedding. He's still my best man.

It took both Sharon and Brean to teach me how to be a dad. I was not a Spock baby myself, and a lot of child-rearing notions had changed since the iron discipline days of my father's generation. I learned things about myself and new sources of joy. The importance of holidays was revived for me in discussions of the appropriate Halloween costume and the assembly of a race car on Christmas Eve. Even Presidents Day was a winner because two feet of snow kept us from going to work that day. We declared it a play day and had a great time.

Sharon loved my work schedule in those days. We could have lunch together and share the office gossip of our respective departments. *All Things Considered* ended promptly at 6:30 PM, leaving plenty of time for dinner out and maybe a movie. Then one day that schedule changed abruptly. On October 27, 1979, producer Jay Kernis stopped by Sharon's desk and said, "I think this will be good for him."

"What are you talking about?" she replied. "What will be good for whom?" That's how Sharon learned that her new husband was going to host NPR's new morning newsmagazine, *Morning Edition*, and start his day at 1:00 AM.

Sharon felt she'd been sucker-punched. I had married her, got her pregnant, and now I was changing the rules. This 1:00 AM alarm-clock wake-up was not part of the deal. What other bombshells awaited her? She never really forgave me for that.

She tried to be a good sport though. On the day of the first *Morning Edition*, Monday, November 5, 1979, Sharon followed me downstairs, cooked me a hearty breakfast of bacon, eggs, and toast, kissed me good-bye, sent me out into the black early morning, went back to bed, and promised herself she would never do anything so supremely stupid again. She didn't.

Susannah was born on April 15, 1980, the perfect present for my parents, who were celebrating their forty-first wedding anniversary that day. Sharon had quit her NPR job the previous month to launch a career as full-time mom, not a popular choice among women of her generation. Among our contemporaries, the stay-at-home parent is regarded as a luxury by couples unable or unwilling to part with that second salary. Given my sleep schedule of 6 PM to 1 AM, having a full-time parent and household manager was a necessity. Someone had to keep sane hours.

I was not an irresponsible parent. I changed diapers, wiped noses, and taught the children how to ride bikes. I was there for the soccer games, the dance recitals, and the parent-teacher conferences. But the heavy lifting of child-rearing is in the emotional nurturing, and those deep discussions that reassure a troubled young person seemed to happen late at night while I was asleep. Fortunately, those chats were Sharon's specialty.

To Sharon fell the burden of grocery shopping, cooking, cleaning, and laundry. She got the cars repaired, the plumbing fixed, and the house painted. She went through three station wagons, hauling children thousands and thousands of miles to games, practices, parties, classes, concerts, and destinations now long forgotten. Meanwhile, I had a career.

When they were little, the children had a phrase for those times when I would put on a suit and tie and go make speeches and raise money for stations. They'd say, "Oh, Daddy has to go be Bob Edwards." At home, I was Daddy. In public, I was Bob Edwards. Sharon made it possible for me to be Bob Edwards.

Sometimes the division of labor was ludicrous. In 1983, *Morning Edition* went on the road to Los Angeles for a week. An ambitious schedule of interviews had been set up for me at the LAPD, Beverly Hills High School, the set of *Hill Street Blues*, and other interesting venues. I took the family with me so they could have some fun while I was busy being Bob Edwards. On the first day, over breakfast, we determined that Susannah, age three, had mysteriously gone blind.

Sharon searched the phone book for a doctor but could find only page after page of plastic surgeons. So while I was off "doing" Hollywood, Sharon and Susannah were in the emergency room of a hospital where the poor of southern California go to be ignored. Doctors were too busy treating the victims of gang shootings to bother with a white, middle-class blind girl. After a couple of days of this, Susannah finally got a CT scan, a lumbar puncture, and a diagnosis. It was a virus, and her vision eventually returned. And where was I while Sharon was dealing with this horrible family crisis? Well, I was at the Playboy Mansion interviewing Hef.

Just when I thought Sharon had assumed all the responsibility she could handle, she found more to do. Our third child, Eleanor, born in 1985, turned out to be a girl who loved learning but hated classrooms. She felt that classrooms were places for rowdy kids obsessed with clothes, cliques, and popular culture. Classrooms were not fit for Eleanor's education, so she was homeschooled after the fourth grade. I gave this project no chance to succeed and even worried that it would destroy a close mother-daughter relationship. Clearly I underestimated them, as both found it a rewarding experience.

Naturally Sharon wondered how it might have been had she made a different choice. This usually occurred when some well-shoulder-padded female professional snubbed her after hearing the answer to the question, "And what do *you* do?" What did she do? Just about everything.

On the day she was called to work at NPR, Sharon also got an offer from the American Film Institute. Had she chosen AFI, she might have ended up with some Hollywood hunk, spending her free time lunching with the swells and flirting with the pool boy. Instead, she cleaned the cat boxes in our basement.

On November 5, 1999, *Morning Edition* celebrated its twentieth anniversary with highlights from past programs, updates of stories covered over the years, and some nice things said about the host. The highlight of that program was an essay Sharon wrote and read on the air:

For twenty years, *Morning Edition* listeners have been telling me they wake up every morning with my husband. I hardly ever wake up with Bob Edwards, except when the alarm clock goes on for too long. Living upside down for twenty years—nearly half my life—was not my choice. No social life. No dog—might bark. Shhh! Quiet after Bob's 6 PM bedtime. Our three kids are as boisterous as monks. Halloween on a work night becomes a tactical nightmare. Bing-bong. Trick or Treat! Then—Oh, no! Christmas carolers! Quick! Head 'em off at the corner! You get the idea. But it's all worthwhile, because every so often I get to go on the road with Bob. Over the years, *Morning Edition* listeners have welcomed us into their homes and communities in places far outside the Beltway. Bethel, Alaska, leaps to mind, with its colorful, above-ground sewer pipes and two-by-four lumber sidewalks. John and Kathy McDonald were there with their sled dogs. *Morning Edition* listeners don't seem bound by television and shopping. They percolate with imagination, humor, and creativity. Hmm. A fellow named Yegen, who raises beef cattle near Billings, Montana, showed us the family museum that contains, among other curiosities, the "world famous" two-headed calf. Listeners are surprising, like Scott, a carpenter from the Blue Ridge who's studying for an advanced degree in ornithology and carries Roger Tory Peterson around in his pocket. One year we chain-sawed firewood with listeners Tom and Jean Sutherland at their cabin in the Colorado Rockies. Tom had been held hostage by terrorists in Beirut for six-and-a-half years—a horrifying ordeal that might have discouraged lesser folks—but Tom and Jean are enchanted by their world, astonished by and grateful for their incredible lives. And they thought Bob was the bee's knees. Kent and Sharon Marlor of Rexburg, Idaho, took us to a chuck-wagon dinner (beans and barbecue) and to a live performance of a melodrama—*I'll save you, Little Nell.* Then we toured Yellowstone with a Mormon geologist named Ed, who, with his wife, had adopted thirteen children. Listeners have generous spirits.

I can keep going. Bill Brooks in Anchorage. Alan and Marcia Baer in Omaha. Ellen Stallworth in South Carolina, whose baby, Hal, must be nearly twenty now. Jim, Sarah, and Martha Foster in Oregon, friends from the beginning. Toby Wells and his bunch at Lake Waccamaw. Bobbie the riot girl and Roger the dog whisperer in Kentucky. Little Guy Black and family. Jack Hillerich, who makes baseball bats, and Watts Auman, who grows peaches. There are many more, but you probably want to hear the rest of *Morning Edition.* Congratulations on being the best, most interesting audience Bob could ask for. Thanks for the memories. I hope I'm privileged to meet the rest of you in the next twenty years.

It was a splendid essay, sincerely expressing just the right sentiments. What made it special to the occasion, though, was that it brought the listeners into the anniversary celebration. The quality of the audience was the best part of working at NPR. It was a challenge to get up in the morning and go to work for an audience like that. Sharon remembered the listeners.

Sometimes Sharon had to remind me how lucky I was. When PBS rebroadcast the NBC series *I'll Fly Away,* it ran the shows on Friday night, one of two nights each week when I got to stay up with the grown-ups. I marveled at the series, which was so well-written and beautifully acted. I told Sharon that I envied Sam Waterston and Brenda Taylor for being part of a company of skilled artists dedicated to doing a job so well. I said, "Whatever else they do, they can look back at this project and say, 'I was a part of that team.'" Sharon said, "Can't you say the same thing?" She was right on the money again.

I thought we'd grow old together, but Sharon ran out of patience with me. In the spring of 2009, as we were approaching our thirtieth anniversary, she told me she'd had enough. We agreed that our marriage hadn't failed because it had produced those fabulous children. I was lucky to have had her in my life for so long.

PILOT ERROR

———

The commuting hours became radio's prime time once TV captured the nighttime audience. That's why *All Things Considered* is broadcast during the late afternoon and evening rush hour. It took NPR nearly a decade to launch a major program in morning drive time, when the radio audience is even bigger.

Morning Edition was the dream of NPR president Frank Mankiewicz, programming vice president Sam Holt, and news vice president Barbara Cohen (now Barbara Cochran). In 1978, they hired a consultant, Larry Lichty, and formed a planning committee of NPR reporters and producers. These dozen or so people were the sole supporters of *Morning Edition*. The rest of us at NPR wanted nothing to do with it—indeed many were hostile to the very idea of a second big program.

Since its first broadcast in 1971, *All Things Considered* had defined NPR. It was not the only program we had, but it was the focus of all our attention and most of our precious few resources. Those of us on the *ATC* staff in the late seventies were proud of the program and very protective of it. We saw *Morning Edition* as a potential threat—not only to our status as NPR's premier program but also as a drain on the limited money, material, and energy NPR had at that time. It wasn't just jealousy on our part. We feared NPR would end up with two mediocre programs instead of the one great one it already had. Staff reporters shared our concerns. They put no faith in management's promises that *Morning Edition* would somehow provide its own material with no help from the NPR reporting staff. The reporters knew they would end up filing stories for both programs—limiting what they could do for either.

Mary Tillotson and Pete Williams were hired to host the new program. Ted Landphair was hired as executive producer and Mark Kuhn as producer. Landphair was highly respected in the Washington market. His news department at commercial station WMAL (then number one in Washington) had won numerous awards. But Landphair's very first moves at NPR foreshadowed the doom ahead for *Morning Edition*.

I suspect Landphair had some kind of chip on his shoulder regarding newspeople at NPR. I believe he regarded us as a ragtag bunch of kids unworthy of the professional world, for his first act was to initiate a dress code. Today NPR has people who know a gown from a smock, but to impose a dress code on the 1979 staff (still being paid in the teens) was like putting tuxedos on the homeless. Some of our people had two outfits—good jeans and bad jeans.

At a *Morning Edition* staff meeting, Landphair stood before a flip chart and bellowed, "Here is my title." Then he flipped the chart to reveal the word BOSS. "And here," he continued, "is Mark Kuhn's title," flipping again to a chart that read BOSS WHEN I'M NOT AROUND.

You may well imagine the state of morale on *Morning Edition*. Boy, was I glad not to be part of that crew! I was even beginning to feel sorry for the people we had seen as a threat. My attitude turned to smugness in October 1979 when the *Morning Edition* staff finally got around to producing a pilot program.

The long-awaited pilot was heard on our in-house speaker system and relayed to eager station managers by closed circuit. It was, by unanimous account, a bomb. Susan Stamberg and I listened in our office. I recall laughing a lot, both at the pilot we were hearing and at the expression on Susan's face, a sort of shocked, "Am I really hearing this?" kind of look. The new program may have been a threat to our resources, but it wasn't going to surpass us artistically.

The word many used to describe the pilot was *commercial*, which I think was intended to give Landphair some of the business he had given us. As one who began in commercial radio, I felt that calling the pilot too "commercial" was an insult to all the honorable men and women who had worked in commercial broadcasting for the previous sixty years. The word I used was *chatty*. One heard chatty hosts yammering on and on about trivia. It sounded like bad, small-market TV. To broad-cast a program like that to a public radio audience accustomed to hear-ing a substantive *All Things Considered* would have been disastrous.

It's important to remember that this was a pilot, not a program broadcast over the air to the public. In roughly that same era, the TV networks put their awful trial runs right on the air. ABC's debut of *20/20* was a howler. NBC launched a magazine program in which a re-porter tried to interview a woman whose face was obscured by a large hat. It turned out she didn't speak English anyway. CBS tried and failed with a program emulating, of all things, *People* magazine. Bombing in private isn't so bad. Embarrassing yourself before millions of people is humiliating.

NPR was not going to be humiliated. If heads didn't exactly roll, they at least disappeared from the newsroom. Ted Landphair and Mark Kuhn were fired—along with their dress code and flip chart. The hosts were fired too, on what may have been the luckiest day of their lives. Pete Williams and Mary Tillotson probably owe their long, lucrative TV careers to being canned by nonprofit NPR.

There was an all-staff meeting at which our leaders told us they were committed to debuting *Morning Edition* on November 5, then only days away, because stations had already promised their listeners there would be this great, new wonderful program that day. An executive shed tears—never a pretty sight. One young woman got caught up in the emotion of the moment and exclaimed, "Don't worry, we'll all help out." But an *ATC* veteran muttered, "Keep your mouth *shut*!"

All this drama was only mildly interesting to me because my ener-gies were focused on a big project. I was producing a story on the fifti-eth anniversary of the stock market crash, scheduled to take the entire middle half-hour of *All Things Considered* on October 29. It was to be a major opus featuring interviews I had done with economists and histo-rians, memories of the Depression from our listeners, music from the early thirties, and the obligatory "Can it happen again?" segment. It was an ambitious project and, as it turned out, my farewell to five years on *All Things Considered*.

On the big day, I was running behind. In order to make the deadline, I farmed out part of the production to Art Silverman. I was typing out a final script when my little office suddenly got very crowded. I looked up and saw Barbara Cohen, *ATC* executive producer Chris Koch, and Rick Lewis, who was on the *Morning Edition* planning committee. This could not be good news. These people were about to change my life.

Barbara asked me to host *Morning Edition* for just thirty days while she searched for permanent replacements for Pete and Mary. She made all the appeals to team spirit, etc., but I had never thought the *Morning Edition* people were on my team. They were going to hurt my team— the *All Things Considered* team. I glanced at Chris for clues. Should I go over to work for our in-house rival? He was no help, a completely blank face. My story deadline loomed and I needed to get these people out of my office so I could finish my script. "Thirty days? Okay." I figured if I helped them out of a jam, they'd owe me one.

NPR executives were up against the wall. There was just one week to go before the scheduled debut of *Morning Edition,* not enough time to bring in more new blood from outside. Their only option was to draft recruits from existing programs and go with proven people who knew how to put on a program worthy of the *All Things Considered* audience. Frank Fitzmaurice, producer of live events, replaced Ted Landphair. My new cohost was Barbara Hoctor, who had been hosting *Weekend All Things Considered.* Jay Kernis, who was supposed to be the arts producer for *Morning Edition,* got the bump to producer in place of Mark Kuhn.

We had one week to right the wrongs, master a difficult format, get acquainted with our new mates, find talented contributors, and deliver an effort that would impress listeners and station managers. It was not impossible, provided there were no last-minute surprises. On November 4, the eve of the first broadcast, we got our last-minute surprise. Radical Islamic students seized the U.S embassy in Teheran and took more than fifty American hostages. We were not yet equipped to respond to a major overseas story, so the first program's only mention of Iran occurred in the newscasts of Jackie Judd and Carl Kasell.

The major adjustments for me were in the pace and format of *Morning Edition.* A *Morning Edition* story is shorter than an *All Things Considered* story, and there are more of them. The program moves faster than an afternoon program, reflecting the faster pace of listeners on their way *to* work instead of on their way *from* work, when the urgency factor is less intense.

The format of the program, ten modular segments plus newscasts and shorter interludes along the way, was a great departure from *ATC*. Whereas *ATC* was meant to be a continuous ninety-minute broadcast from Washington to our member stations, *Morning Edition* consisted of two hours to be *shared* with those stations. We at NPR would fill both hours with news, but the stations didn't have to air all our material—they could break in at many various points in the program and substitute local news, weather, sports, headlines, and traffic reports. This meant the timing of each segment, and each story within a segment, had to be precise. Stations intending to insert a lot of local material were counting on us to begin and end each segment when we had promised.

I made my peace with the format right away. It was too bad that not all the stories and interviews I was doing would be heard on all the stations, but that was the format and there was nothing I could do about it. Besides, I was going to do this program for only thirty days, right? Ah, hindsight. If I had known I was going to have to listen to the tape of that first program on every *Morning Edition* anniversary broadcast for the next twenty-four years, I would have taken more care with the first introduction.

At first, the "open" to each hour was ninety seconds. That's much too long, and it was later shortened to a minute. We hosts were not allowed to use the opens in the same way that *ATC* hosts used their "billboards," to tell listeners what they were going to hear on the program. We could not promise that listeners would hear a given story because a station might be running a local segment in place of that story. It was also pointless to put headlines in the opens because the opens were followed by newscasts. So the opens on the first day's program sounded like trivial gibberish. I told listeners it was Guy Fawkes Day and the beginning of National Split-Pea Soup Week and other such nonsense unworthy of a serious national news program. I cringe every time I hear a recording of it. Producer Jay Kernis ultimately came up with the solution. The opens would be used to billboard the day, rather than the program. I started telling listeners what events were expected to occur during the day just beginning.

We were not heard in all the major markets that first day. Some nervous station managers feared we would not improve on the pilot.

Others were reluctant to abandon the classical music they'd been playing every morning for decades. The stations that carried us were pleased, and NPR management was thrilled. We had turned an off-air failure into an on-air success in barely more than a week. Congratulations were extended, champagne was poured, and souvenirs were distributed.

Before my thirty days were up, I decided to remain with *Morning Edition*. I had always envied the Linda Wertheimers and Susan Stambergs who had been with *All Things Considered* since its debut. Here was a challenge—to launch this new program and someday make it as good and as popular as *ATC*. It was a bit of a risk. *ATC* was a proven commodity, a program that was going to be around forever. There were no such guarantees if I cast my lot with *Morning Edition*.

DISASTER

Morning Edition celebrated its first anniversary in the same week that voters chose Ronald Reagan to be the fortieth president of the United States. For NPR management, Reagan's election was ominous because Pat Buchanan and other ideologues were part of the Reagan team. When he had served on the Nixon White House staff, Buchanan had been the point man in a successful campaign to kill public television's attempt to launch a national news production house. Public television was still trying to realize its potential beyond arts performances, children's programming, and cooking shows. The National Public Affairs Center for Television (NPACT) was launched in hopes of making public TV a force in news programming. Buchanan and cohorts saw it as the one part of the media mix they could destroy. Public broadcasting was still heavily dependent on federal funds in those days. By marshaling opinion against NPACT and threatening a presidential veto of money appropriated by Congress, Buchanan could intimidate public broadcasters into dropping the project. He portrayed NPACT correspondents Sander Vanocur and Robert MacNeil as Nixon-hating liberals who were being paid $100,000 and $65,000, respectively. Buchanan figured working-class voters would be appalled at such sums, though they were extremely modest by network news standards even then. Buchanan's propaganda was outrageously false yet effective. NPACT didn't last long, and public television has never had a national news production house to do for public TV what NPR has done for public radio.

The Buchanan crowd in the Nixon White House left NPR alone. I don't think we were significant enough then to be on their radar screen in the early 1970s. By the time Buchanan returned to the White House with the Reagan administration in 1981, we were a very different NPR. Millions listened to us and knew our broadcasts had integrity. *Morning Edition* had raised NPR's profile. Commuters could now start their workday hearing NPR news on their drive to the office and again on *All Things Considered* while driving home. Buchanan knew about us, and given his history, there was reason for NPR, still heavily dependent on federal funds, to be paranoid.

There was no way to insulate NPR from political attack or attempts to intimidate us, but NPR management felt something could be done about the reliance on government subsidies. The law allows nonprofit organizations to engage in profit-making ventures provided the profits support the nonprofit activities. NPR president Frank Mankiewicz announced that NPR would "enter every profession except the oldest one." NPR would make money leasing excess satellite capacity to broadcasters and other commercial users. Partnerships were formed with companies developing satellite paging systems and a device that would program a radio to record programs in the way a VCR taped TV programs. (In 1981, these were technological marvels still in our future.) These are the projects I remember, but there were others.

While launching these business ventures in 1983, Mankiewicz also greatly expanded news and arts programming. The plan was for NPR to grow bigger and stronger, the growth to be financed by the revenue from the commercial ventures.

It's the nature of journalists to ask questions, and the journalists who worked for Frank Mankiewicz asked many questions of him at staff meetings called to explain and "celebrate" the launch of the new ventures. Had he or any member of his management team had experience in the business world? Wouldn't these ventures require some capital investment by NPR? Where would NPR, an organization limping along on a budget of several million dollars, get such funds? What was NPR's liability if the ventures failed? Don't most start-ups have to endure a few years in the red before recovering their investment and turning a profit? If so, where were the reserve funds? Was there a backup plan if the ventures tanked? Would the failure of the new businesses affect our traditional broadcasting of radio programs? We reporters were not business geniuses; our questions were fundamental and based on curiosity, prudence, and a bit of nervous anxiety. Managers of NPR member stations asked these same questions and more. All our questions got the same answers. The ventures would pay for themselves; they could not fail and there was no risk to NPR.

They failed. They failed spectacularly and with deep, long-lasting consequences. The ventures were undercapitalized and their start-up was delayed. The pipeline was too long, and money was going out with no revenue coming in to finance the expanded radio programming. Nothing had been done to insulate NPR from suffering such a fate. In just a few months, NPR had incurred a debt of more than seven million dollars. It would have been more had the ventures not been ended and the bleeding stopped when the seriousness of the situation was discovered.

In most commercial businesses, seven million dollars is not considered a debt but rather a small setback, a minor reversal that works itself out without too many questions from stockholders. But at a nonprofit outfit such as NPR, seven million dollars is an enormous sum, and in 1983, nearly equivalent to our annual budget. The financial disaster nearly killed NPR.

Members of Congress demanded a full explanation. Some station managers were so furious as to suggest that public radio would be better off without NPR. The general public was angry about tax money being squandered. Some listeners were upset because they felt we had misused the money they had given us during pledge drives. The life of a nonprofit organization depends on public goodwill. Once the confidence of supporters is shaken, it's difficult to regain. It mattered little that the money was merely misspent, not extorted.

The guilty were fired, of course, but not before many innocent people lost their jobs to reduce costs (some returned later in healthier times). Station managers decided to continue *Morning Edition* and *All Things Considered*, but little else. Most other news programs and nearly all our arts programs were ended. Some of the people who survived the layoffs decided it was a good time to give up on NPR and work elsewhere.

New business procedures were introduced, and the smallest purchases were scrutinized. Replenishment of office materials was suspended for a time. When we exhausted our supply of paper for the newswire teletype machines, we borrowed paper from the CBS Washington bureau across the street.

Those of us who had such big dreams about what NPR might become had to recalibrate those dreams with NPR's very existence in doubt. Morale sagged, but I tried to be upbeat when Bryant Gumbel interviewed me for *The Today Show*. Camera crews were regular visitors at NPR in those days. We journalists love disaster stories, and NPR covered this one too. Scott Simon had the thankless task of covering NPR's financial crisis on NPR.

Ironically, there was a benefit from our misery. Thanks to the attention we got, some people heard about NPR for the first time and became regular listeners. The cliché is that there's no such thing as bad publicity as long as they spell your name right. A certain gallows humor set in when I taped an interview with Blackstone, the magician. I asked if he could make a seven-million-dollar debt disappear. He replied, "Sure," and then we played the effect that sounds like a xylophone arpeggio. If only it had been that easy!

Producers, editors, reporters, and hosts struggled to make do with less, and we managed pretty well. Freelancers suffered because we had to stop buying their work. We had to make the work produced in-house last longer on the air. We did that by cutting back on the editing. Instead of running two or three stories over a nine-minute block of airtime, we now ran only one long one.

We also ran multipart interviews, most successfully in the case of Jack Paar. Paar, the former host of *The Tonight Show* on NBC, was promoting his memoir in 1983. Normally, I taped a half-hour interview with an author, and listeners got to hear the best five, six, or seven minutes of that half-hour. In the case of my Jack Paar interview, listeners heard almost every word. We "stripped" it, running portions every day in the same time slot for a whole week. The material sustained itself because Paar was such a great storyteller and we could augment the interview with clips from his old shows. In fact, he was so good that we probably would have run it in two parts under normal circumstances.

Station managers were ambivalent about NPR, angry with management but supportive of staff who worked so valiantly under awful circumstances to keep the programs on the air. Some workers figured we were doomed and took their annual leave in anticipation of NPR's imminent end. They looked like the wise ones on the day we were told there was no money to meet the next payroll. We were asked to work in good faith, hoping that something would be worked out by payday. That looked like a sucker's bet at the time because we were reading the angry comments of station managers every day in the *Washington Post*.

It came down to this: I left work on a Thursday believing that the next day would be the very last *Morning Edition* and there would be no Friday paycheck for my final two weeks with NPR. I did not prepare a farewell to read to listeners but figured on saying something simple: "NPR has been a noble, usually splendid experiment in broadcasting and journalism. Like you, we're sorry it has to end. Thanks for listening. Good-bye."

When I arrived at 2:00 AM for that "final" broadcast, I learned that we were still in business and we'd even get paid that day. While I had been asleep, a deal had been worked out by NPR management, a group of NPR station managers, and officials of the Corporation for Public Broadcasting (CPB). The stations would pay off the debt through a loan from CPB.

There were cuts in public broadcasting funding during the Reagan years but no all-out assault of the type that had killed NPACT years earlier. Perhaps Buchanan and company figured we would perish from self-inflicted wounds. That prospect did not seem out of the question in 1983.

There were people at NPR who never forgave Frank Mankiewicz for bad judgment and reliance on poor advice that took the network to the brink of death. I completely understand those feelings, but I think Frank's failure has to be balanced against his accomplishments. His first act was to recognize AFTRA, ending the patronizing attitude of NPR management toward its employees. Frank was instrumental in changing the formula for funding public broadcasting so that radio got

25 percent of the federal appropriation. Prior to that, radio had to beg for the scraps left over after public TV had taken most of the money. Forward funding began on Frank's watch. The annual congressional appropriation became a two-year appropriation, allowing NPR and its stations to know two years in advance how much money they were going to get and to plan accordingly. Under Frank's leadership, NPR became the first national broadcast network to distribute all its programs by satellite. *Morning Edition* is part of Frank's legacy. The volume of positive press attention he brought to NPR, its programs, and its staff was something we had not known before he came to NPR and never again enjoyed to that degree.

The fallout from the financial disaster of 1983 endured for many years. Much of the spirit that characterized our early years evaporated. We lost our innocence. Boldness disappeared too. We became unwilling to try anything remotely risky. Stations had to be reassured that NPR was not going to do anything that would cost them money or cause them embarrassment. Opportunities were lost or deliberately passed over. Our public relations staff was dismissed. I got the feeling that management wanted little or nothing said in public about NPR.

That malaise lasted into the 1990s. Some residual effects were still obvious when NPR entered the new millennium announcing ambitious plans for programs produced for new media, online, and direct satellite broadcasts. Yes, new ventures financed by a profit-making subsidiary. Once again, staff meetings were called to explain the ancillary activities. The same doubts were raised and questions asked all over again, especially by the people who had asked them in 1983. Déjà vu? No, we were told. That was then, this is now. Eventually, the plan for a profit-making subsidiary was shelved.

Then NPR hit the lottery. Joan Kroc, widow of McDonald's hamburger tycoon Ray Kroc, died in 2003. In her will, Mrs. Kroc left $225 million to NPR. It was the ultimate Happy Meal. A gift of that size completely transforms a nonprofit, removing the burden of constantly worrying about survival. Investing a nice chunk of that amount ensured that the gift would continue to make money by paying interest. The money also financed minority training and other worthy projects, and it allowed NPR to open some new bureaus at a time when the rest of journalism was closing theirs.

A few months after they got their money from the Kroc estate, NPR executives removed me from my program. Quite a few listeners who protested my removal suggested the Kroc money had given the executives a financial cushion that empowered them to ignore criticism of their actions.

MORNING EDITION

———

When NPR nearly crashed in 1983, *Morning Edition*, then in its fourth year, was already too strong to be one of the disaster's victims. Before *Morning Edition*, most NPR stations did not even show up in the Arbitron ratings for morning drive time. By the program's first anniversary in November 1980, member stations had seen their morning audiences double, triple, or quadruple. A few had done even better. In hindsight, it's easy to say this success was predictable. After all, NPR was merely inserting a strong news program into radio's peak time slot. Those who would say that have never launched a radio program.

Every new project has a shakedown period, and ours lasted about a year. Producers Frank Fitzmaurice and Jay Kernis received daily feedback from stations, listeners, and NPR staff. Some things worked and some didn't. The opening theme was shortened, and there was some tinkering with the clock, adjusting the points where program segments began and ended.

My cohost, Barbara Hoctor, left the program for personal reasons after just four months, and it was decided she would not be replaced. To the listener, I already had other cohosts—hundreds of them. Since *Morning Edition* was a modular program with local stations cutting in and out of the national broadcast, each station had its own local *Morning Edition* host handling the local inserts. A local host added to two national hosts is at least one host too many. Beginning in March 1980, I flew solo.

A program's voices and the talent, experience, and integrity those voices convey to listeners are crucial to success. We could not have done better than to start *Morning Edition* with newscasters Jackie Judd and Carl Kasell. These masters of a difficult and demanding craft allowed me to extend my personality on the air. If I got too far "out there" with some feature story, Jackie and Carl returned the listeners to the solid, professional sound of NPR news.

An impressive cast of commentators and other contributors added their voices and talents to the mix. Award-winning sportswriter Frank Deford was with us at the beginning and so was critic Tom Shales of the *Washington Post*. Deford happily has remained with *Morning Edition*, though he dropped out for a couple of years to edit *The National*, an experiment in daily sports-magazine journalism. Ideally, we would have Shales end every Friday broadcast with one of his brilliant, witty movie reviews. He left the program because the burden of being one of the most important TV critics in the country left him precious little time to watch movies for NPR.

The early years of *Morning Edition* had a literary sound. Writers Doris Grumbach, Rod MacLeish, and Ellen Gilchrist delighted our listeners, as did the late John Ciardi. Ciardi was a fascinating man, surviving World War II as a tail gunner aboard bombers. He translated Dante and became one of the most important American poets of the twentieth century. He had a great sense of humor and loved language, trading limericks with his pal Isaac Asimov. For *Morning Edition*, Ciardi served as etymologist, seeking and commenting on the derivation of words and idioms. Listeners loved him, and he involved them in his work, promising to send one of his *Browser's Dictionary* volumes to the listener who could find for him the source of a word or phrase. He paid off too.

For political commentators we had social critic Michael Harrington as a sort of liberal conscience. Kevin Phillips served in the Nixon White House, but he was (and is) too fair and open-minded to be a slave to ideology. Peter Osnos, then of the *Washington Post*, analyzed politics, and

Lou Cannon, who had covered Ronald Reagan's California gubernatorial years, was invaluable to us during Reagan's two terms as president. Our most beloved commentator was sports-broadcasting pioneer Red Barber. We developed holiday traditions. Holidays are slow news days, so a program needs to fill the airtime with good material appropriate to the occasion. Chuck Kramer, a commentator for a Boston TV station, was one of the original commentators on *Morning Edition,* but he quit after providing only one commentary. It was a poem that lamented the commercialization of Christmas by listing every trendy brand-name gift Kramer could imagine. He had to update it several times, but it ran every Christmas for twenty years.

Producer Alice Winkler took care of Thanksgiving for us. She created a textbook piece of radio production. It was a nine-minute fantasy in which the most famous chefs in America came to my house—each one bringing his or her contribution to the Thanksgiving Day feast. She did all the interviews herself and then wrote a script for me that made me sound as though I were talking with each of the guests. Throughout the piece, one hears the sounds of a genial group of guests having a wonderful time. It ran for years until one of the chefs died. Then Neva Grant produced a new version with different chefs and less traditional cuisine.

My favorite holiday tradition was the Independence Day brainchild of Sean Collins. It was a reading of the Declaration of Independence by dozens of voices from the NPR family. It began with me, saying the familiar "When in the course of human events . . ." Then Carl Kasell picked up the reading at the "We hold these truths to be self-evident" point. Jean Cochran read next, then Cokie Roberts, and so on, ending with me again. Ted Clark, Susan Stamberg, Renee Montaigne, Baxter Black, Red Barber, and many others were heard along the way. The reading took eight-and-a-half minutes, perfect for one of our nine-minute segments. It stirred me every time I heard it, reminding me that every brave soul who signed that document took the risk that it would be his death warrant if the British quashed our revolution.

Sometime in the 1990s, I decided to read the names of all NPR military veterans in the *Morning Edition* closing credits on Veterans Day. I figured that would be easy enough to do since I could think of only four others besides myself. When I asked the whole NPR staff if there were any others, I got thirty more. I was proud to read all those names each year.

Retired general and former test pilot Chuck Yeager helped us cover the launch of the first space shuttle. While *The Right Stuff*, Tom Wolfe's book on the Mercury astronauts, had revived interest in Yeager, NPR apparently was the only news organization that thought to use his expertise for the shuttle launch. The TV networks had their big, expensive, air-conditioned trailer complexes in place for launch at Cape Canaveral and for landing at Edwards Air Force Base in California. The NPR broadcast facility at Edwards consisted of Yeager and correspondent Neal Conan sitting at a card table in the desert. When the TV networks learned of our coup, they sent limos to the card table in hopes of whisking Yeager off to more comfortable digs and a respectable fee. To his eternal credit, Yeager waived them off and honored his commitment. You've got to like a general who's loyal.

Yeager not only knew about flying but sounded great talking about it in his fabulous West Virginia accent. Producer Jay Kernis, a Yankee from New Jersey, loved Yeager's accent so much that he had the general patched in to my Friday talk with Red Barber. So Yeager of West Virginia was talking with Barber of Mississippi and Florida, and I undoubtedly sounded more Kentucky than I had in twenty years.

For another of my conversations with Yeager, Kernis hooked us up with Arthur C. Clarke, author of *2001: A Space Odyssey*. Clarke was speaking from his home in Sri Lanka and was difficult to hear in those days before satellite telephones. It could have been the static, or maybe Yeager was not a big science-fiction fan, but halfway through the conversation on how the shuttle program might affect the future of space travel, Yeager passed a note across the card table to Neal Conan. The note read, "Who the hell am I talking to?"

Live interviews were numerous in the early days of *Morning Edition*. Executive producer Frank Fitzmaurice favored live interviews with Washington political types because they are the easiest guests to get and the interviews would help raise our profile among the movers and shakers. I talked with so many members of Congress that the staff called the segment "Meet the Member." Some of the guests were still on their way up, including Vice President George Bush, Governor Bill Clinton, and Representative and later Senator Al Gore, plus Newt Gingrich, Tom Foley, and Richard Gephardt, who were on the program long before they became leaders in Congress.

There is always a danger that live interviews will backfire, such as one I did on Election Day in November 1980. Fitzmaurice had me interview the grand old patriarch of Dixville Notch, New Hampshire. Dixville Notch is a village of just a few dozen souls who, on every Election Day, employ a gimmick to get their town mentioned on radio and TV stations across the country. The town votes at midnight on Election Day and closes the polls ten minutes later, after all the town's eligible voters have exercised their Constitutional privilege. Then for many hours they get to hear newscasters say, "The first results from this year's election are official. In the town of Dixville Notch, New Hampshire, . . ." So on Election Day 1980, I interviewed an eighty-something fellow who had been up late voting and hadn't had enough sleep. He spoke in that terse New England way that regards the waste of a syllable as a mortal sin.

> ME: "Well, who'd you vote for?"
> HIM: "Reagan."
> ME: "Why?"
> HIM: "Liked him."

It was a classic example of what questions *not* to ask if an interviewer wants to elicit an insightful response. As a Bob & Ray routine, it was hilarious. As a live interview that wasn't meant to be funny, it had me breaking out in a sweat. I think listeners heard several minutes of music to fill out the segment.

I did a lot of interviews concerning Britain's war with Argentina over some South Atlantic islands called the Falklands by the British and the Malvinas by the Argentines. NPR was still not sufficiently bankrolled at the time to send multiple correspondents to world hotspots. I had a daily, three-way conversation with NPR's Robert Siegel in London and Chris Hedges, who was based in Buenos Aires for the *New York Times*. The British ambassador to Washington visited the studio for an interview and was impressed with the big Falklands map we had hung over the couch, which laughingly passed as the "greenroom" at our old M Street offices. Engineer Jim Schelter taped some cartoon sheep to the map. Sheep far outnumber humans in the Falklands. Before the Argentine ambassador arrived for his interview, Schelter pasted the word *Malvinas* over the word *Falklands*.

Our penurious condition didn't last too long. We found the funds to cover the wars in Nicaragua and El Salvador. Soon we were placing full-time staff correspondents in Europe, Asia, Africa, and the Middle East. I recall a conversation with NPR's William Drummond as he stood on his hotel balcony in Beirut describing an Israeli air strike, the planes and explosions quite audible as he spoke.

NPR did some of the earliest reporting on AIDS. Science correspondent Laurie Garrett, who'd done graduate work in immunology, was reporting on the disease before it had its acronym and was still only a number. For this we earned not the thanks of a grateful nation but rather the scorn of people who were tired of hearing us talking so much about gay men, the population group hit hardest by HIV.

In 1982, public radio stations in Alaska got their satellite uplink, which allowed them to do statewide programming for the first time and to send reports to the Lower 48. Both *Morning Edition* and *All Things Considered* celebrated this milestone by doing a week of programs from Alaska. Noah Adams flew in a balloon near Mt. McKinley. Wendy Kaufman visited an offshore oil platform. Howard Berkes covered commercial fishing. I talked with an Eskimo family and went salmon fishing on the Talkeetna River with my producer, Jay Kernis. Laurie Garrett interviewed a social worker about the effects of the long winter isolation on people living in the bush.

A big story in the eighties was the fall of President Ferdinand Marcos in the Philippines, a crisis that began with the assassination of popular Senator Benigno Aquino upon his return home from exile. As the Philippine government began unraveling, we made nightly attempts to reach Marcos for an interview. Associate producer Joe Smith managed to get hold of a Marcos aide who was perhaps not all that savvy about the pecking order of American media.

MARCOS AIDE: "Who did you say you're with?"
SMITH: "National Public Radio in Washington."
AIDE: "You are *the* national radio in America?"
  (*one-second pause*)
SMITH: "Yes, that's right. We are *the* national radio."

The aide brought Marcos to the phone and I had my interview, thanks to the quick-thinking Joe Smith. I have considered NPR *the* national radio of America ever since.

Marcos was defeated by Aquino's widow, Corazon, and Aquino's younger brother, Agapito, visited Washington to win support for the new government. Before taping an interview with the young Philippine legislator, I asked him to carefully pronounce his first name so that I could say it correctly on the air. Then he had to listen to me rehearse it: ah-gah-PEE-toe, ah-gah-PEE-toe, ah-gah-PEE-toe. When I got to about the sixth or seventh rehearsal, Agapito Aquino said, "Oh, just call me Butch. Everybody does."

Searching for Easter eggs in my backyard. This passed for excitement in the Eisenhower years (photo courtesy of Loretta Edwards).

My high school senior yearbook photo in 1965. I was already begging radio stations for a job.

At twenty-one I was a rookie broadcaster at my first station in New Albany, Indiana.

PFC Edwards doing sports for AFKN-TV in Seoul, while SP4 Mike Pope takes a break from the news.

Editing audiotape in the analog era. Our irreverent comment on that early *All Things Considered* poster was "turn your head and cough" (photo courtesy of Barbara Isard).

Flannel shirts and jeans have always been my favorite radio clothes (photo courtesy of Barbara Isard).

Anchoring *All Things Considered* coverage of the 1976 Democratic National Convention in Madison Square Garden in New York. *Left to right*: Michael Weiss, Robert Nathan, David Molpus, David Creagh, me, Ceil Muller, and Robert Krulwich.

The 1977 staff of *All Things Considered* in the office of executive producer Jim Russell, who obviously chose his own clothes back then. *Back row, left to right*: Jon "Smokey" Baer, Jim Russell, Jackie Judd, Jack Mitchell, Bob Saunders, me, Susan Stamberg, and Cathy Primus; *front row, left to right*: Joe Oleksiewicz, Claire Etheridge, David Molpus, David Creagh, Noah Adams, and John Morello (photo courtesy of Barbara Isard).

Meeting on the beach in Newburyport, Massachusetts, in the summer of 1977 with Ed Bliss, my professor, mentor, friend for thirty years, and the most important person in my career (photo courtesy of Barbara Isard).

With Susan Stamberg, my *All Things Considered* cohost and mentor. This 1979 photo was commissioned by TIME Magazine for a feature story about NPR (photo courtesy of Dennis Brack/Black Star).

In happier times with *Morning Edition* senior producer Jay Kernis in the early 1980s. I truly believed we were mutually supportive good friends.

I couldn't get an interview with Jimmy Carter when he was president. Now that he's an author, we talk almost every year.

With *Morning Edition* producer Katherine Ferguson and recording engineer Gary Henderson in the office of Vice President George H. W. Bush. Years later I interviewed his oldest son, who was running for president.

Interviewing Vice President Al Gore for *Morning Edition*, with recording engineer Michael Cullen (photo courtesy of Molly Bingham).

At home in Arlington, Virginia, in 1986, when all the pieces still fit together (photo courtesy of Stan Barouh).

The host of *Morning Edition* clearly had somewhere to go that day in June 1990—either a speaking gig or a power lunch, judging by the adult clothes I'm wearing (photo courtesy of Diane Uhloy).

Concluding the only face-to-face broadcast Red Barber and I ever did, in Tallahassee, Florida, on October 19, 1990 (photo courtesy of Bob O'Lary Photography).

A host of public radio hosts—Carl Kasell, Ray Magliozzi, Ray Suarez, Terry Gross, Tom Magliozzi, and Susan Stamberg.

Garrison Keillor got me to join him in singing a jingle about toasted soybeans for the May 29, 2004, broadcast of *A Prairie Home Companion* at the Wolf Trap National Park for the Performing Arts in Vienna, Virginia.

Edward R. Murrow was born on a farm beside Polecat Creek east of Greensboro, North Carolina.

Ed Chapman and Ken Greene at my NPR farewell party. Chapman, a George Washington University freshman, collected more than twenty-six thousand signatures on an online petition demanding that NPR retain me as host of *Morning Edition*. Greene is the AFTRA representative who negotiated the terms of my resignation from NPR.

With actress Morgan Fairchild at my NPR farewell party. Morgan and I are members of the AFTRA national board.

My National Radio Hall of Fame induction on November 6, 2004, a day after *Morning Edition*'s silver anniversary without me. I went into the Hall as a satellite radio broadcaster. No one from NPR attended.

The original staff of *The Bob Edwards Show*—Phil Harrell, Melissa Gray, Tish Valva, Chad Campbell, me, Mark Schramm, Andy Danyo, and Ed McNulty—posing with a photo of Red Barber on the day of our first broadcast, October 4, 2004.

Interviewing actors Grant Heslov, George Clooney, and David Strathairn about their Edward R. Murrow film *Goodnight and Good Luck* (photo by John Harrington).

Reporting on immigration and watching an arrest in the Arizona desert north of Nogales, Mexico, in January 2006. I'm with recording producer Geoffrey Redick and Dr. Bob Cairns of the Samaritans humanitarian group (photo courtesy of Michael-Hyatt.com).

With actor Philip Seymour Hoffman, who appeared on *The Bob Edwards Show* in January 2006 to promote the film *Capote*, for which he won an Oscar (photo by John Harrington).

On writer Wendell Berry's farm in Henry County, Kentucky, with recording producer Geoffrey Redick (photo courtesy of Andy Danyo Kubis).

Interviewing Randy Newman on March 30, 2007, before a live audience at the Paramount Theatre in Seattle to benefit public radio station KPLU.

The Bob Edwards Show staff on our third anniversary, October 4, 2007, bonding in shirts designed by the host. *Left to right*: Steve Lickteig, Dan Bloom, Geoffrey Redick, Andy Danyo Kubis, Chad Campbell, Sam Wright, Shelley Tillman, Ariana Pekary, me, Cristy Meiners, and Ed McNulty.

With Carl Kasell and Jean Cochran. The longtime *Morning
Edition* trio reunited in Chicago
for Carl's 2010 induction into the
National Radio Hall of Fame.

Vacationing in Florida in April 2010 with daughters Susannah and Eleanor, aka Moon-
beam and Sunshine.

My hometown features murals of native sons and daughters, such as Colonel Sanders, Diane Sawyer, Louis Brandeis, and Muhammad Ali. Mine is on Baxter Avenue in the Phoenix Hill section of Louisville (photo courtesy of Geoffrey Redick).

RECONSIDERING ALL THINGS

Remember in 2000 when Governor George W. Bush became the Republican nominee and Dick Cheney was given the job of vetting possible running mates for Bush? Alone one day in his office, Cheney conducted a room-wide search and found the perfect guy for the job—himself.

Not to compare my good friend Robert Siegel to Dick Cheney, but he did something similar. It happened in 1987 when Robert was the NPR news director.

The story begins in St. Paul, Minnesota, where Garrison Keillor had become a celebrity way beyond his comfort level. A local paper published his address, and he was getting drive-by attention that he took to be a major invasion of his privacy. Garrison decided to drop his fabulous program, *A Prairie Home Companion*, leave St. Paul, and have a major-league midlife crisis. Minnesota Public Radio replaced Garrison's program with *Good Evening*, hosted by Noah Adams, who had my old job as cohost of *All Things Considered*. So who would replace Noah on *ATC*? I thought it should be me.

I went to see the news director, Robert Siegel, and told him I wanted to return to my former post. Who could do that job better than one who had performed well in that position for five years in the seventies? It would reunite the old team of Susan Stamberg and Bob Edwards. I'm sure I suggested it might be a little reward for having established *Morning Edition*, which was then in its ninth year. I had paid my dues—now could I please resume normal sleeping hours? I probably mentioned my children, then ages twelve, seven, and two—and wouldn't it be nice if they could see Daddy in the evenings? What I didn't know is that Robert wanted the job.

It would be fun to say that once I left his office, Robert Siegel, now alone, made a room-wide search and found just the right fellow for the job—himself. Nope, Robert has more style than Cheney. He told me the decision would be made by the producer of *All Things Considered*, Ted Clark. I went to see Ted, who, as my *ATC* editor years earlier, really helped me focus my interviews. I respected Ted a great deal and poured out for him the same spiel I'd delivered to Robert. It turned out that there was a second thing I didn't know: Ted wanted to be a reporter, and the guy who could make that happen for him was the news director. So each of these guys could give the other what he wanted. The cards had been dealt, but I had no hand to play.

I like Robert and I like Ted. I'm telling this story because I think it's funny. I don't know when I reached that conclusion, because in 1987 I wasn't laughing.

NEWS LEADER

By the 1990s, NPR had recovered financially and was firmly within the circle of the most authoritative providers of news in America. The decade would see the TV networks shift their energies from daily news coverage to prime-time magazine features and celebrity interviews. Taking their place was the Cable News Network, able and willing to cover breaking news anywhere in the world at any time of day. C-SPAN now covered the political news conferences and congressional hearings once available only on NPR. United Press International was in critical condition, no longer a worthy wire-service competitor of the Associated Press. Fine old family-owned newspapers were gobbled up by the chains, making the *Washington Post*, *New York Times*, and *Wall Street Journal* more vital than ever. As for radio journalism, NPR stood alone, offering two-hour newsmagazines morning and evening seven days a week, opening bureaus in the United States and overseas while expanding newscasts to a twenty-four-hour-a-day schedule, and starting a midday program, *Talk of the Nation*.

It's a good thing we were ready for the nineties because the decade's events were exciting. I don't know one fellow baby boomer who expected to outlive the Cold War. Back in the eighties when Lech Walesa and the Solidarity movement challenged the Polish government (and by extension, the Soviet Union), we feared they might be crushed as effectively as those involved in the Hungarian uprising of 1956 and the

"Prague Spring" of 1968. Instead, Solidarity's success inspired the rest of Eastern Europe, and the dominos falling this time were the Communist governments. Pieces of the Berlin Wall were dispersed throughout the world as souvenirs. Independent republics emerged from the Baltics to the Balkans, and the Russian people prepared for the first elections they'd ever known. I have never taken such pleasure in reporting events to an audience.

In those early post-Soviet days, NPR's Brooke Gladstone filed a story on Russia's Vladimir Orphanage three hours from Moscow. The star of her report was a seven-year-old boy named Vova, whom all the orphanage personnel adored but who had been impossible to place for adoption because he had a number of physical impairments. Rick Stafford heard that story while driving to his job in Cincinnati. "When I heard his voice," Stafford recalled later, "and when I heard him singing, I just knew he was to be our boy." Stafford and his wife, Diana, traveled to Russia, adopted the boy, and gave him a new Kentucky home.

There was more good news from Africa with the end of apartheid. Majority rule was achieved in Rhodesia (now Zimbabwe) and South Africa. Unfortunately the stories from the rest of the continent were about war, famine, and disease.

The Persian Gulf War brought many new listeners to NPR. We were able to send up to a dozen people to the region, thanks to a war chest amassed by our vice president for news, Bill Buzenberg (with major contributions from member stations such as KCRW in Santa Monica and WBUR in Boston). One of those reporters, Neal Conan, spent a week as a prisoner of Iraq's Republican Guard.

President George Bush's nomination of Clarence Thomas provided legal affairs correspondent Nina Totenberg with a scoop that topped the many she had during the Iran-Contra period. Members of the Senate Judiciary Committee holding confirmation hearings on the Thomas nomination were told that an unidentified former associate of the nominee accused him of sexual harassment. Committee members were happy to ignore this information until Nina convinced Anita Hill to go public with her accusation in an NPR interview. Feminists and other liberal Democrats opposed to Thomas's judicial philosophy demanded that Hill be called as a witness at the confirmation hearing. Hill's testimony and Thomas's rebuttal were so dramatic that even the television networks carried those sessions live. Thomas was confirmed, but congressional Republicans never forgot that Nina and NPR brought Anita Hill out of the shadows. They subpoenaed Nina's phone records, but she fought that action and won.

Bill Clinton was elected and had his health care initiative hammered by Congress. Republicans used that victory as a springboard to take control of Congress in 1994. NPR won an Alfred I. duPont-Columbia Award for coverage of the Republican revolution. Our Washington reporters and editors did all the heavy lifting, but one of my bit parts in that coverage is a moment I treasure. I did a live interview with Dick Armey, who was to be the new majority leader in the House, and I asked him about the "contract with America," a successful gimmick the Republicans had used in their campaign. I recited the points in the contract and asked Armey how he would implement them. When we got to term limits, Armey said the American people would be so thrilled with the new Republican majority that term limits would not be an issue. I nearly spilled my coffee when he said that, because term limits had been an important issue in the campaign. In fact, I once had to separate a Congressman and a lobbyist who nearly came to blows in my studio during an argument over term limits. Just to make sure I heard him right, I asked Armey a follow-up question and got the same answer. The Associated Press was listening and immediately put out a story. The *Washington Post* reprinted Armey's comments, and several conservative columnists ripped the presumptive majority leader. His phone must have been ringing all day. Armey then backpedaled, announcing his support of term limits in a press release under this headline in bold type: "The Danger of Talking to NPR Early in the Morning."

One of the major Republican campaign promises was to reduce the size of the Washington government bureaucracy. One of their big targets was the Department of Education, but eliminating an entire cabinet department would take time. They needed a scalp real fast—something that was easy pickings—a federal agency they thought no one would fight for. They chose the Corporation for Public Broadcasting (CPB), the agency that channels federal funds to public radio stations and other recipients.

This was the very blow that Frank Mankiewicz had feared four-teen years earlier, but even if the Republicans had been able to follow through on their plan, the blow might not have been fatal. Public radio had changed its funding structure so that NPR received no national programming funds directly from CPB. That money now went straight to the stations, which used the funds to buy programs from several suppliers, including NPR. In addition, NPR and its stations had diver-sified its sources of income, relying more on corporate grants, foun-dations and especially listeners. (The taxpayers' share of many station budgets today is just 15 percent.) Still, the loss of CPB funds would have been a blow.

This was not just an idle threat; it was a fight the Republicans en-tered with enthusiasm. Newt Gingrich, destined to become Speaker when the House convened, threatened to use "the power of the gavel" to kill CPB. He promised he "will not even recognize a member who rises to propose funds for public broadcasting."

Revenge was likely one motive for targeting CPB. Congressional Republicans could not get over the Clarence Thomas confirmation flap and often mentioned Anita Hill when asked about the move to axe CPB. They also greatly underestimated the popularity of public broad-casting, which, after all, was about much more than NPR news. Public broadcasting was the *News Hour, Car Talk, Wall Street Week, A Prairie Home Companion, NOVA, This American Life,* and *American Masters.* More than anything else, however, public broadcasting was about little preschool rug rats sitting down in front of the children's programs on PBS. Two generations had been raised on *Sesame Street.* Barney and Big Bird became symbols of the battle. In a match between stuffed ani-mals and stuffed shirts, always bet on the bird.

There's an NPR member station in just about every congressio-nal district. Those managers marshaled listeners into a fighting force to let Congress know how they felt about public broadcasting. They also visited Capitol Hill along with Mary Lou Joseph, who would be-come NPR's vice president for national affairs, and Delano Lewis, who stepped in to the NPR presidency at this very crucial moment.

It was not much of a contest. In fact, it was a rout. Members of Con-gress were suitably impressed by the reaction of public broadcasting fans. They not only dropped plans to kill CPB but modestly increased its funds. For all of us within public broadcasting, the public support we received in 1994–95 was immensely gratifying.

The battle over CPB funding did not distract us from continuing with our mission. NPR distinguished itself in covering the many conflicts in the Balkans, winning the Overseas Press Club Award. Tom Gjelton and Sylvia Poggioli were superb in their reporting. *Morning Edition* supplemented this fine coverage with a compelling subplot involving two high school kids and their email.

In the late nineties, *Morning Edition* hooked up with Youth Radio, a Berkeley, California, outfit that tries to interest young people in radio and vice-versa. It was a good arrangement that gave our listeners some exposure to how high school students regard the world. Working with Youth Radio was a young man named Finnegan Hamill. From his church group, Finnegan received the email address of a teenage girl in Kosovo. Their correspondence, which Finnegan shared with *Morning Edition* listeners, was fascinating. The Kosovo girl, an apolitical ethnic Albanian, went by the pseudonym Adona to protect herself and her family. Her emails, read superbly by Youth Radio's Belia Mayeno Choy, were just what we needed to hear. Adona hung out with a group who wanted nothing to do with the ancient conflicts of their ancestors. She was realistic about the threat from Serbs but longed for a new society in which Serbs and Kosovar Albanians could get along. Finnegan was magnificent, writing of his sympathy and understanding, acknowledging that it was hard to square his San Francisco Bay–area life with what his email pal was enduring. He wanted to do more—but what? He was doing plenty, of course, by sharing this correspondence with American radio listeners, personalizing troubles we couldn't otherwise feel for faceless people who had a lot of consonants in their names. With the Serbs closing in, Adona and her family had to go into hiding and the emails stopped. Listeners worried. Was she okay? Weeks passed before we heard from her again. Kosovo was occupied by international troops and the Serbs were on the run. We could now report that Adona had a real name, Kujtesa Betullahu, and she was coming to America on a student visa. The series, titled "Letters from Kosovo," won a duPont-Columbia Award for Youth Radio.

Morning Edition in the nineties featured political analysis each Monday by Cokie Roberts, who couldn't quite leave NPR completely behind when she moved to ABC News. T. R. Reid of the *Washington Post* was another important contributor. Reid is a natural storyteller and superb on the radio. I loved the commentaries contributed by Pat Morrison of the *Los Angeles Times* and Judy Muller of ABC News.

In 1997, NPR sent me to London, where Mark Schramm, Michael Cullen, and I joined our bureau staff for coverage of Princess Diana's funeral. After the service, we walked the streets of a city in mourning. People were drinking in the pubs, but they were silent. Diana's home, Kensington Palace, was surrounded by people who had left flowers and mementos covering vast acres of the grounds. The Britain of the stiff upper lip was history. The new Britain of Tony Blair was a nation that cried.

In 1999, Carl Kasell and I went on a national speaking tour to celebrate the twentieth anniversary of *Morning Edition*, and celebration was appropriate. For many years, *Morning Edition* had had more listeners than any other public radio program and more listeners than any of the morning network TV programs had viewers. Public radio stations raised more money from *Morning Edition* listeners than they did from the listeners of any other program. That's not bad for a program completely rebuilt from the ashes of failure barely a week before its debut.

In the middle of the twentieth anniversary celebration, *Morning Edition* received the Peabody Award. It was a fitting way to end the millennium and start a new one.

OVERNIGHT

In my *Morning Edition* years, I went to a different NPR member station each month for some sort of fund-raising activity. It was good politics to help the stations, but I had other reasons for going. Telling people about *Morning Edition* was good marketing. It also allowed me to meet the audience that brought me into their homes, cars, and offices—and it was useful to find out what was on their minds.

The public radio audience is intelligent. Who but an intelligent, concerned person is going to bother listening to a two-hour program that's serious about the news? So I always expected that when I opened the floor to questions, someone would ask me about monetary policy and the Federal Reserve Board. Fortunately, that never happened. Instead, my listeners wanted to know anything I could tell them about our Rome-based correspondent Sylvia Poggioli, or they'd ask, "What time do you have to get up in the morning?"

My alarm buzzed at 1:00 AM. I kept the alarm on the other side of the bedroom so that I couldn't reach it from my bed. If it were within reach, I might have turned it off without opening my eyes. Having the clock across the room forced me to get out of bed, put my feet on the floor, and walk several steps to reach the clock and silence that sucker! By then I'd be awake, sort of.

Clocks can fool you. Once, I woke up, looked at the digital clock, and thought it read 1:00. If I had read all the digits, I'd have seen that it was only 11:00. Not until I saw the astonished looks of the *Morning Edition* staff did I realize I was at work two hours early. Years earlier, when my clock had the standard round face with the hour and minute hands, Sharon shook me one morning and said, "Bob, get up. It's three o'clock!" I stared at the clock and said, "Honey, that's not three o'clock, that's 12:15. You've got the hands reversed."

Some nights I woke up minutes before the alarm went off. Sometimes Sharon didn't hear the alarm. I dressed in the dark so I wouldn't wake her. That meant I had to lay out all my clothes before I went to sleep so that I knew the location of each item in the dark. Then I reached for the door, careful not to dislodge the bra hanging from the doorknob (I lived in a house with three females—if there was not a bra hanging from every doorknob, I knew that I was on the road alone, staying at a hotel). I was usually fully awake by the time I got downstairs, but not always. Once I grabbed what I thought was the mouthwash bottle but ended up gargling my aftershave. I stopped using a liquid aftershave.

I had a cup of strong, hot, black coffee before daring to drive, and I carried a second cup with me for the trip to work. To increase my chances of getting there in the snow, I bought a four-wheel-drive vehicle, an investment that paid off every winter.

It was only a fifteen- to twenty-minute trip, but it was one of the most dangerous times to drive. I was on the road just after "last call" at the bars. Hardly a night went by that I didn't see a drunk driver. I saw lots of wrecks—and potential wrecks—cars filled with men chasing cars filled with women. I saw drivers weaving erratically, drivers who hadn't bothered to turn on their lights, and drivers going the wrong way on a one-way street. Twice I had drivers come straight at me on the wrong side of an Interstate highway, a very scary situation because the curves and tunnels are not constructed so that drivers can see oncoming traffic. I had to make quick decisions whether to stop or attempt to slip by the oncoming drunk on the left or the right. But which? After all, I was trying to outguess a drunk!

Before the Interstate was built, I was hit by a drunk who ran a red light. She was nineteen years old, had been fighting with her mother, and was on the way to her boyfriend's house. My car, which was totaled, was brand new. I was still driving on the dealer's tank of gas.

This accident happened in the early eighties, before the crackdown on drunk driving. The young woman got off easy. No fine, suspension, or rehab, just a few compulsory movies. I was scheduled that day to interview Sissy Spacek and had her press kit in my car. The crash broke my windows and spun the car in a circle, so that everything inside my car was now outside. Imagine a major suburban intersection littered with eight-by-ten glossy photos of a Hollywood actress. I rushed to pick them all up before the police arrived and took me for a stalker.

While driving to work one night, I looked in the rearview mirror and saw a car moving entirely too fast. I figured it was another drunk and pulled to the side of the Interstate to let him pass. The driver slowed down and pulled up behind me. It was a state trooper who thought I was drunk. A couple of sober paranoids in the night.

Most of the *Morning Edition* staff kept crazy hours, with people arriving or leaving at various times throughout the day. We had young people attempt to have a social life, going out on dates before starting work at midnight. Most concluded this didn't work for them and asked to transfer to the day shift. Some liked the overnight shift because the suits (management) were asleep. There was nearly always some food available. People brought in items they were trying to get rid of and found it worked every time, because overnight workers seem to get the munchies. It was a great place to bring the Halloween candy you didn't want your kids to eat or the candy you had stocked for trick-or-treaters who never called at your door.

Halloween was one of those occasions on which everyone assumed that the homeowner was awake, not sleeping. New Year's Eve and the Fourth of July were other nights on which revelers never considered that someone wanted to sleep until 1:00 AM. Why should they figure someone worked my hours? It's not a normal thing to do.

Sometimes there was an evening appointment I had to keep, perhaps a union meeting or a school function. On those days I took a long afternoon nap. No one thinks a person is asleep in the afternoon. I tried to take precautions. The doorbell had been disconnected and the phone unplugged to keep the telemarketers at bay. That left the garbage truck, the moving van, and the neighbors using a chainsaw on their firewood.

People heard about my schedule and asked, "How do you do it?" I answered, "Not very well." We are not biologically made to keep such hours. It's not something to which one adjusts either. One o'clock in the morning felt lousy no matter how much sleep I'd had. The one adjustment my body *did* make was negative. I find that I can't sleep more than six hours in a row. So if I tried to go to bed at 10:00 PM on the weekend, I'd wake up at 4:00 AM. If I waited until midnight, I'd be up at dawn.

Getting up so early was less a problem than going to bed early. I tried to get there by 6:00 PM, but it wasn't always easy. I had to back-time everything to make certain I could get to bed on time. For example, a station in the Midwest would want me to speak at a luncheon. I had to calculate the length of the lunch, the travel time to the airport, the two-hour flight back to Washington, and the trip to my house. Would it now be after 6:00 PM? If so, I wouldn't be able to get enough sleep to be alert for the next morning's program. Sunday nights were a real problem. There was no way I could wake up at 8:00 AM and feel sleepy at 6:00 PM. The rest of the week was easy. Having awakened at 1:00 AM on Monday morning, it was no problem getting to sleep at 6:00 PM on Monday evening.

Carl Kasell took an afternoon nap, woke up for dinner and a bit of TV, then had a second round of sleep. I couldn't do that, even though my body was begging for sleep after lunch. When I tried sleeping in two shifts, I found I had difficulty going back to sleep for the second shift. So I forced myself to stay awake until 6:00 PM and get that continuous block of sleep.

When my children were little, they'd read me bedtime stories. It was ridiculous being a dad who had to go to bed three hours before the children. I longed to stay up like a grown-up. On weekends, when we switched roles, I'd fall asleep while reading stories to them. They would wake me and insist on my finishing the story so they could go to sleep.

I learned to respect sleep. Sleep is the great healer, a magical remedy that seems to cure or relieve most ailments I get. Sleep restores the body and the mind. When the old folks told us, "Sleep on it—you'll feel better in the morning," they were absolutely right.

Today my alarm clock rings at 5:00 AM. Yes, that's still plenty early, but the obsessive concern over sleeping hours no longer rules my life.

FRIDAYS

———

Back in the 1970s, NPR was the antiestablishment alternative. By the end of the 1980s, we could no longer claim to be the underdog; we were more like the *New York Times* of the airwaves. Our audience mushroomed by millions in the eighties, and I believe there were three reasons for that.

Most NPR stations are FM, so the network was going nowhere until the market demand moved radio manufacturers to offer products featuring both AM and FM. Until then, an AM/FM radio was an option that might cost a car buyer an extra hundred dollars. When AM/FM radio became standard equipment in everyone's car, NPR could finally reach a big audience.

Ronald Reagan, the guy we thought was going to do us in, unwittingly gave NPR a huge boost by partially deregulating radio. Gone was the requirement that radio stations offer minimal hours of nonentertainment programming, with the result that stations all over America promptly fired their news staffs. Radio listeners spinning the dial in search of news found the one place where there was still plenty of it—NPR.

The third factor in NPR's audience growth in the eighties was *Morning Edition*, born late in 1979, and one of its commentators, pioneer radio sportscaster Red Barber. Red's four-minute segment each Friday on *Morning Edition* from January 1981 until October 1992 was the most popular attraction NPR ever had. It ran at a predictable time, 7:35 AM—the moment at which the morning drive audience peaks—and it was live, which gave the conversation even more energy. At that hour, listeners are busy with breakfast, showering, shaving, dressing, commuting—but the *Morning Edition* listeners let none of that interfere with hearing Red. They adored him.

Many of Red's fans in the *Morning Edition* audience cared nothing for sports and had no recollection of his play-by-play work for the Reds, Dodgers, and Yankees from 1934 through 1966. My listeners just loved to hear the music of his Southern accent as he spoke from his house in Tallahassee, Florida, where he'd be celebrating the abundance of dogwoods, azaleas, and camellias in his garden or recounting the latest mischief caused by his cat. Those Friday conversations were the perfect way to end the week.

Red sounded ill in our last on-air conversation on Friday, October 5, 1992. On the following Friday, I told our listeners that Red was in the hospital. The hospital received more cards, letters, flowers, and fruit baskets than it could handle. NPR received get-well cards for Red—enough to fill three large boxes, which are now in my home. Hundreds of listeners described bursting into tears when I told them Red had died on October 22.

Since Red had meant so much to our listeners, I decided to take four months off and write a book about his life, his time on *Morning Edition*, and our friendship. *Fridays with Red* was a nice little book about an old man and a young man—a mentor and his student. The old man is endearing, funny, and says wise things. Then he dies and the young man misses him. It sold forty-two thousand copies and is now out of print.

Four years later, sportswriter Mitch Albom wrote a book about his friendship with college professor Morrie Schwartz. *Tuesdays with Morrie* is a nice little book about an old man and a young man—a mentor and his student. The old man is endearing, funny, and says wise things. Then he dies and the young man misses him. So far it has sold twelve million copies in more than fifty editions around the world. It may never be out of print.

I'm pretty sure no one who reviewed *Tuesdays with Morrie* made any mention of the earlier *Fridays with Red*.

STYLE

As a twenty-five-year-old at WTOP in 1972, I had the pleasure of working with Dave McConnell, who was then anchoring the afternoon drive-time broadcasts. Joking with the new kid in the newsroom, Dave said, "Bob, if you're going to make it in this business, you have to have an act." He used two of our WTOP colleagues as examples: sportscaster Warner Wolf, whose distinctive style made him the most popular broadcasting personality in Washington at the time, and features reporter Doug Llewellyn, who later became Judge Wapner's announcer on TV's *The People's Court*.

"Look at Warner," Dave instructed, "He's got an act. And Doug, he's got an act. Bob, you've just got to get an act."

"Okay, Dave," I replied, "Here's my act. My act is to be the guy without an act."

Dave said, "You can't have that act because it's already taken—that's my act." Dave is a solid reporter who never needed an act. All these years later, he remains with WTOP, covering Capitol Hill.

Dave was kidding, of course. No one successful in radio or TV news has an act. Listeners and viewers respond to people who are just being themselves. Wolf and Llewellyn were effective on the air, but it was a product of their personalities. They weren't acting. They spoke the same way off the air as they did on the air.

A comedian once wondered if TV anchors spoke in private as they do on the air. He imitated David Brinkley, who had an unusual cadence that emphasized the last word in a sentence, and the comedian portrayed Brinkley speaking that way to his wife at home. "Good morning, DEAR. I've been outside to retrieve the morning PAPER. Now I'm enjoying my breakfast of ham and EGGS." Having interviewed Brinkley, I can report that his speech was the same on-air and off.

There are indeed broadcasting personalities who have an act, but they're not in news. Dick Vitale is a good example. Basketball fans either love or hate his outrageous persona on ABC and ESPN, but it's something he chooses to give them. Arriving at NPR for an interview, Vitale was a perfectly normal human being. We quietly discussed a book he had written, and I was on my third question when it suddenly occurred to him that we were not just chatting; the interview was under way. Dick Vitale instantly morphed into DICKEY VEE: "Hey, wait a minute. Is this IT? Are we ON? HEY BAYBEEEEE. LET'S TALK COLLEGE HOOPS NOW!!!!"

The cowboy singing trio Riders in the Sky never dropped their act when they visited my studio. They were in character from the time they stepped out of the elevator until they got back into the elevator half an hour later. Nothing I said on microphone or off could break them out of their routine of being cowboy musicians and comedians. They spoke warmly of their love of entertaining all the little buckaroos in their audience and told me they'd see me down the trail.

I don't have an act—but I have a style. One important element of my style is minimalism. I say what I have to say in as few words as possible. This goes back to my early days as a newscaster, when telling a story in the fewest possible words allowed me to tell more stories in my allotted five minutes. It's not the way to become a memorable broadcaster in a medium that values people who can use words to paint pictures in the listener's mind, but it serves a purpose. I believe the news is more important than I am. I'm the messenger, not the message. Now that I'm an interviewer and not a newscaster, I suppose I'm a bit chattier, but I still feel that my listeners want to hear from my guests, not me. If I'm talking, my guests are not speaking. The less one hears of me, the more one hears from my guests. Consequently, my best interview questions are brief retorts such as "Really?" "No kidding" "Well?" and "No!" Each of those is a signal to my guest that he or she is saying something interesting and should speak more about the subject.

My writing is simple, direct, and spare—also a product of my years writing newscasts—and it has the advantage of not wasting the listeners' time. My listeners are smart, but they are listening to me while doing other things, such as driving a car or preparing school lunchboxes for children. If I tell them a story without a lot of unnecessary words, my listener has less data to process while multitasking on the way to work. The listener retains more because my words have not imposed a gratuitous burden.

This was known as "Bobspeak" to the *Morning Edition* staff who wrote and edited much of what I said. If the scripts were not in "Bobspeak," I'd change them before I read them on the air. New staff members had to learn not to use wire-service words that one never uses in conversation: curb, stem, spur, thwart, and the like. I told them that *curb* is what they should do with their dogs. They knew they should avoid unnecessary adjectives and adverbs because these are words that can color the story. If I say that a Senator "boldly and defiantly" confronted his critics, I may be giving you an accurate account of what he did, but I also sound like I'm taking the Senator's side against those carping critics. The Senator's critics rightly would say that my fingerprints were on that story.

Clichés are my enemy, and sometimes I don't catch them in time. I feel humiliated when I hear myself saying something as stupid as "The president handed Congress a political hot potato this week." He did? Are there photos? The oldest journalistic cliché story is about the reporter covering the Johnstown flood who, overcome by the horrible devastation, led his story by writing that "God stood on the banks of the river and wept today." His editor cabled back, "Forget flood, get pix of God." My journalism professor, Ed Bliss, joked that we should "avoid clichés like the plague." Clichés make reporters sound stupid and lacking in imagination for not giving better descriptions.

Jeffrey Neuman, who edited my first book, didn't care for my terse sentences. He may have thought I was trying to imitate Hemingway, who learned to be spare with words (Papaspeak?) during his early career in journalism. Jeff introduced me to the colon and said, "Look, you can use one of these to incorporate two different thoughts in a single sentence!" I think I used four or five to make him happy.

I honestly don't know how the *Morning Edition* staff felt about "Bobspeak" because I was afraid to ask. I hope my former coworkers knew that I respected and admired them very much and didn't mean to burden them with my preferences for clear, clean copy. I feared they might believe my quirks were the product of an egomaniacal host who was star-tripping. There are good reasons for my idiosyncrasies, but I can't always take the time to explain them. It's important to know that *Morning Edition* sounded best when I was reading with confidence, knowing that verbal snags were not waiting in the next sentence to trip me. They must have understood that, but I wouldn't be surprised to hear that they always looked forward to my vacation. On the other hand, Rod Abid remembers handing me news copy that referred to "the biggest dam project in Asia." He says I caught it and fixed it. If that sticks in Rod's mind, maybe he thought I was okay.

Another "Bobspeak" no-no is anything that attempts to be cute or clever, thereby making the host (me) sound like I'm full of myself. Remember the reaction Mary Richards got from Lou Grant when she wrote such a lead? "That's cute, Mare. I hate cute."

The closest I get to cute is the occasional frivolous final question that lets my guest get in a closing punch line of his or her choice. Wrapping up an interview with TV chef Julia Child, I asked if she'd ever had a Big Mac. "Actually, I prefer the quarter-pounder," she replied.

To actress and later ambassador Shirley Temple Black: "Do you ever get tired of hearing "On the Good Ship Lollipop"?

"No. That's my SONG."

Who's the worst person to interview? Is it a cliché-spouting professional athlete or a politician paying no attention to the question he or
she has been asked? I think it's the politician.

Obviously, interviews regarding public affairs are crucial to any
news program, but for the very reason that they deal with the news,
they flunk the "memorable" test. The news is, by definition, transitory.
A news story is already old once it's been broadcast. We often follow up
on stories that have dropped out of the headlines, but usually we move
on to something new. Political interviews are important at the time,
but that time passes.

I certainly do remember my interview with President Clinton because it was my only visit to the Oval Office. Waiting for the president
to arrive, I made mental notes on what books were in the room, the pattern of the upholstery, and the variety of stuff on the president's desk.
Impressive, but not as nice as Martin Sheen's office on *The West Wing*.
I recall that Clinton was headed for his budget showdown with Congress and used a buzzword common to Washington dialogue. "If there's
going to be a train wreck," he said, "then it won't be my fault; it'll be the
fault of Republican leaders in Congress." In hindsight, that was an important comment. The "train wreck" occurred when Congress refused
to pass the budget, shutting down many government services. Voters
blamed the Republicans, and their anger helped Clinton win a second

term. It's possible that Clinton foresaw that this would happen when he made that comment to me. If I could do that interview over again, I'd ask him about his intern.

My interview with former Minnesota senator Rudy Boschwitz was memorable because he is, so far, the only person to put me on hold during a live telephone conversation. He had Call Waiting and apparently found the little audio signal too distracting to continue our conversation. Listeners heard me saying, "Senator?" Senator Boschwitz?" He was only gone for the few seconds he needed to blow off his other call, but those were the longest seconds of my broadcasting career. In the next election, he was the only incumbent senator to lose. I did not mourn his loss.

Politicians are seldom memorable interview subjects because they're too guarded. The interviewer is hoping that the conversation will make news. The politician being interviewed is determined to stick with the message of the day, coveting the exposure but making certain to keep the good stuff under wraps. Politicians are under enormous pressure to get through an interview without screwing up. A mistake in an interview can be costly. Ask Dick Armey.

Maybe I've worked in Washington too long, but sometimes I even feel sorry for political figures. While serving as President Reagan's secretary of labor, Raymond Donovan was indicted for grand larceny and fraud. Donovan went on *Morning Edition* to defend himself. This occurred in those glorious years when one could smoke in the studio. Donovan and I each had a cigarette going, but then he lit another one. Now he's smoking two cigarettes to my one. He's got one in the slot on the ashtray corner and another one in his hand. This naturally draws my attention to his hands, which are shaking. After Donovan was acquitted, he asked, "What office do I go to to get my reputation back?" Rarely does a Washington figure get off the hook once there's a hint of scandal. I hope Raymond Donovan is enjoying his retirement.

I don't want anyone to be nervous about talking to me. Yes, I'm going to ask the tough questions that need to be asked, but I don't want anyone to know that. I want my guests to be completely at ease. The more relaxed my guest, the more forthcoming that guest will be. The confrontational style that worked so well for Mike Wallace does nothing for me. Wallace played district attorney and nailed his subjects with questions that might begin with "Isn't it true that on the night of August 3rd in 1982...?" One with anything to hide would be an idiot to talk to Mike Wallace. I often wondered why anyone spoke to him. If I had seen Mike Wallace coming in my direction with a camera crew, I would have run like hell. My approach is the exact opposite. I've interviewed people who didn't know they had just been interviewed. They were so comfortable that they thought they'd been having a preinterview chat with me. No, that was the interview. Of course, Mike Wallace was enormously successful—so who am I to second-guess him?

Occasionally, I'm the nervous one in an interview. This happens when a guest arrives with a large entourage, spoiling the intimacy of a one-on-one interview. I'm not comfortable talking to someone in the presence of handlers who are reviewing the guest's performance and mine too. A party leader from Northern Ireland showed up with an army of aides and three camera crews. I hadn't planned to be on British and Irish TV that day, and I didn't like the fact that a foreign audience that night would see an interview I was taping for the next day. By contrast, only a couple of aides accompanied Vicente Fox when the Mexican presidential candidate visited NPR. We had a good chat about trade, drugs, immigration, and how he treated his workers when he ran Coca-Cola in Mexico. I was impressed by his candor and thought it was too bad that a guy like this had no shot at ousting the party that had ruled Mexico for more than seventy years. Fox won, of course, keeping intact my record at fortune-telling.

Politicians aren't much fun to interview until they've left office and don't mind speaking frankly. Unfortunately, they've lost their news value by that time. I couldn't get an interview with Jimmy Carter during his four years in the White House, but he's been very accessible in his career as our best ex-president. He's also my listener and once heard me announce it was Rosalynn's birthday, an occasion he'd forgotten that year.

When elected officials visit, it's often a chore to get them into the studio because they feel they have to shake the hand of every person they encounter on the way. They're always running for office, always working the room.

If they can't be fun, they can at least be funny. During the 2000 campaign, I asked Pat Buchanan how NPR would fare in the Buchanan administration. He replied, "You'll be National *Commercial* Radio."

During that same campaign, I interviewed Governor George W. Bush, who was trying to be a regular guy and have us forget he went to Yale. So I asked if he was disappointed that his daughter Barbara was bound for New Haven. "Oops, gotta go," he said. And he went.

James Watt, the former Reagan administration secretary of the interior, arrived in Washington with a chip on his shoulder, and it stayed there. Watt never passed up an opportunity to tell the world how much he hated journalists. Perhaps that's why I've never seen an editorial praising him as a great statesman. Watt would never have given me an interview except that he needed to publicize the book he wrote after leaving office. In our conversation, I asked him if he might have accomplished more as secretary of the interior if he'd been less abrasive. Instead of answering, Watt decided it was time to leave. He said, "Thank you very much. Don't edit this too much." Then he got up from his chair and left the studio. I thought his exit was the perfect example of the abrasiveness to which I had alluded, so I asked that it be left on the tape when the interview was broadcast. I wanted listeners to share the James Watt treatment. Weeks later, a *Morning Edition* listener told me that on the day of the broadcast, he saw Watt at a drug store in Washington and asked him, "Why did you walk out on Bob Edwards?" Then Watt walked out on him.

FAVORITES

Musicians and writers are my favorite interviews because they seldom conceal anything. Their songs and novels often spring from the best and worst moments of their lives, and if they can talk about happiness and pain in music or in a book, most don't mind talking about it in an interview.

Disappointed by a Norman Mailer novel, I summoned the courage to ask him if he hadn't just fired off a potboiler. I used the word courage because it's risky asking a provocative question of a man who was once notorious for punching people in the nose and stabbing his wife. Mailer didn't flinch. "Oh sure," he said, "I needed to pay some bills."

Willie Nelson is another honest man, regardless of what the IRS says. Interviewing Willie aboard his tour bus, pungent with the aroma of good weed, I asked him about accidental plagiarism. He said that he had only recently realized that he was among the guilty. An old song popped into his head and he realized the melody was very similar to the one he used for "Crazy," a big crossover hit he wrote for Patsy Cline back in the fifties. Willie said, "I've been singing that song for more than forty years without thinking of the earlier tune."

Some of the best interviews veered off in interesting directions I hadn't anticipated. I asked jazz pianist Dave Brubeck about his version of "Brother, Can You Spare a Dime," in which he plays the signature phrase in different piano styles—rag, bop, stride, even baroque. He avoided the opportunity to brag about his virtuosity and spoke instead about the lyrics. Why do the lyrics matter to a pianist who doesn't sing? He said an artist can't do justice to a work unless he keeps the spirit of the tune, and this one meant so much more because it was about the Great Depression. Then he recalled his rural boyhood home and his mother giving food and shelter to drifters in exchange for chores performed. How very different from our distrust of strangers today. A bit later, he apologized for letting his mind wander. He explained that the previous evening's PBS documentary on the Battle of the Bulge was still on his mind because he had fought in that horrible battle. I knew Brubeck was going to give me a fabulous music interview, but his memories of the Depression and World War II were a rich bonus. *Morning Edition* ran that interview in two parts.

George Shearing, another jazz pianist, gave me an equally fine history lesson just two weeks later. Shearing talked about playing in London during the Blitz, when all lights had to be turned off. Blackouts meant nothing to a blind pianist. Once the "all clear" sounded, people trying to return to their homes had difficulty because familiar landmarks had been bombed. Shearing escorted them home. All his mental landmarks were still intact.

My job has given me the chance to meet many of the rock 'n' rollers whose music formed the sound track of my youth: Carl Perkins, Chuck Berry, Carole King, Fats Domino, Otis Williams (sole survivor of the original Temptations), Curtis Mayfield, Ben E. King, Jerry Butler, Don Everly, Jerry Garcia, Jesse Colin Young, Bill Wyman, Leon Russell, Mark Knopfler, Mike Love, and Little Richard, who told me he was "the king and queen of rock 'n' roll."

Little Richard recalled playing London and having the then-unknown Beatles for an opening act. Backstage, he taught Paul McCartney how to do that high-pitched WOOOO sound with his voice. I thought of playing that tape years later when I interviewed Sir Paul, but the interview took place at a fund-raiser for cancer research and it seemed more appropriate to have him remember his late wife, Linda. Someday I want another opportunity with McCartney so I can ask him how he and John Lennon came up with all those great songs.

Musicians obviously are ideal for radio; even if the interview fails, you still have the music to play. *Morning Edition* listeners were treated to musical interviews with Tony Bennett, Patti Page, Maxine Andrews, Waylon Jennings, Ralph Stanley, Ricky Skaggs, Joe Williams, Frank Patterson, Nancy Wilson, Pee Wee King, Bonnie Raitt, Joe Pass, Illinois Jacquet, Emmylou Harris, Skitch Henderson, Rupert Holmes, Loretta Lynn, Leonard Slatkin, Glen Campbell, and many more.

Placido Domingo told me he does not sing in the shower. I think he does.

Sometimes my admiration for a musician can backfire. Randy Newman is so talented and so funny that when I talk to him, I do more fawning than interviewing. I end up raving over chords that are elementary to a conservatory-trained performer such as Newman. Then, after a couple of his sardonic verbal asides, I start laughing at everything he says. I'm obviously having a great time, but I'm not sure the listener is having the same experience.

Carol Kaye has had a long and highly successful career as a session musician in Los Angeles. On *Morning Edition*, she re-created her parts on the Beach Boys' "Good Vibrations," the *Mission Impossible* theme, movie music, and scores of hit records. It's impossible to listen to the radio, watch TV, or go to the movies and not hear the work of Carol Kaye, yet she's content to remain out of the limelight.

Poets are good on the radio too. My poet guests have included the Nobel laureate Seamus Heaney and young Davis McCombs, who wrote poems about Mammoth Cave National Park in Kentucky, where he gave tours. Maybe I like poets because they cover the whole range of human emotion with very few words. Paul Zarzyski, a former rodeo rider ("I travel the laureate *and* lariat circuits"), recited a poem about a bronc named Moonshine that left him "toothless in Missoula." The late Roland Flint could not bear to read a poem about his young son, whose tragic death he had witnessed, so I did the reading. The audience response to Flint's work was phenomenal.

When Ronald Reagan was elected president, novelist John Gardner told me it would affect books and movies. Gardner predicted there would be more of what he called "redemptive endings" to stories. Sure enough, he was right. There was a period in the early eighties in which the bad guys always got caught, the boy got the girl, and everyone lived happily ever after. Four years later, Reagan's reelection slogan was the treacly "It's morning in America." It couldn't last, of course. Cynicism and irony reigned again long before Reagan left the White House.

Morning Edition listeners are good readers, and they responded warmly to interviews with John Updike, Alice Walker, Philip Roth, Maya Angelou, E. L. Doctorow, Toni Morrison, Garrison Keillor, Lee Smith, Wendell Berry, Nadine Gordimer, William Golding, Grace Paley, Peter Taylor, Bobbie Ann Mason, Pat Conroy, Marsha Norman, Richard Bausch, Mary Lee Settle, and Frederick Busch.

I'm glad I got to my favorite nonfiction writers before they died. Steven Ambrose retraced the path of Lewis and Clark for his book *Undaunted Courage*. Journalist Howard K. Smith shared stories from his autobiography, including confrontations with the Gestapo, a narrow escape from Berlin, a stormy interview with Churchill, and being listed in *Red Channels*, a publication from the blacklisting era. Writer Alistair Cooke told me how, as a young student in Germany, he saw Hitler speak on a street corner in Munich. Cooke said Hitler was such a mesmerizing speaker that the Nazis always had nurses nearby to treat young women who fainted. He made a Hitler speech sound like Beatlemania. Cooke surprised me in other ways too. As host of public television's *Masterpiece Theatre*, Cooke was the epitome of the cultured English gentleman, so knowledgeable and genteel. That image made me forget that Cooke was really a journalist. In my studio he was the journalist Cooke, using salty expressions and chain-smoking Trues, a person who might have shocked viewers who knew him only as the fellow lecturing on Thomas Hardy or George Eliot.

For listener response, it would be hard to top an interview with Bob Greene of the *Chicago Tribune* about his book *Duty*. The book concerned Greene's relationships with two World War II veterans in Columbus, Ohio: Greene's father and Paul Tibbets, pilot of the Enola Gay and commander of the unit that dropped two atomic bombs on Japan in August 1945. As his father was dying, Greene befriended Tibbets and found that he could have all the great conversations with Tibbets that he never seemed to be able to have with his father, especially conversations about the war. Listeners wrote to say how moved they were by Greene's story, though others felt I needed to hear their opinions about the bomb. There always seem to be a few people who hear an interview I didn't do.

Mary Previte told her war story on *Morning Edition*. The daughter of missionary parents, Previte was a child at a British school in China. Her parents were away when the Japanese invaded and forced the children to march to an internment camp. At the end of the war, the camp was liberated by seven Americans who dropped into the area by parachute. Decades later, Previte was a state legislator in New Jersey when she decided to locate her liberators and thank them. It took her a while, but she visited all five surviving veterans and the widows of two who had died. She told me this story with rich detail and genuine emotion. I also interviewed two of her heroes, who said they worried more about the parachute drop than they did about getting the Japanese to surrender. They had not jumped since flight school.

The most gripping war story belonged to Jack Kuhn and Leonard Lomell, two veterans who helped us observe the fiftieth anniversary of D-Day. Their assignment on June 6, 1944, had been to land on the beach, make the long run across the beach through machine gun fire, use grappling hooks to scale a cliff while Germans on the cliff fired down at them, and after reaching the top of the cliff, to knock out the German artillery up there. To me, that qualifies as a suicide mission. Kuhn and Lomell just saluted, went off to Normandy, and obviously lived to tell the tale. They were given a mission impossible and they accomplished it. Another storyteller on that anniversary broadcast was Harold Baumgarten, who was wounded five times on D-Day. Brave men such as those always tell me, "Others did just as much." That's not false modesty; there were many others who performed impossible feats requiring great courage. That they returned from those life-and-death situations to quietly live out their lives as auto mechanics, salesmen, and assembly plant workers is somehow even more amazing to me.

One more interview stands out. William Diggs ran a museum housed at a high school in Charles County, Maryland. It was a museum devoted to slavery, and all the objects in the museum were cruel mementos kept by Diggs's slave ancestors. He had the bill of sale by which his grandmother was sold and the ball and chain once attached to his grandfather's leg. Diggs explained that a runaway, after getting a severe beating, would be shackled with the heavy ball to make it more difficult to try another escape. Diggs's grandfather, though burdened with the extra weight, had to keep up with the other field hands if he wished to avoid another beating. Then Diggs described his grandfather, dragging around this glaringly visible sign of his loss of manhood, trying to court his grandmother. The interview made me see slavery much more vividly than it appears in history books. I call it the Anne Frank effect. Our minds can't fathom six million Jews killed because the number is too great to have meaning. It's the death of that single child that makes us feel the Holocaust in all its depravity. Likewise, we can't relate to tens of millions of human beings enslaved in our own country, but a man's grandmother sold like chattel and his grandfather struggling for some dignity while dragging that heavy ball tells me an old story in a more personal and compelling way. Producer Loretta Williams (with engineer Kevin Rice) turned that interview into a Gabriel Award–winning story called "Bill of Sale."

MEMORIES

NPR made it possible for a working-class kid from Kentucky to go places and meet people I could never have imagined. One of my first NPR interviews outside the studio was at the home of diplomat Averell Harriman. Waiting for him to get off the phone with some potentate or other, I had a look around his place in Washington's Georgetown neighborhood. All around me were items collected from a long lifetime of service: swords, vases, chests, urns, and pistols—gifts from Stalin, Churchill, kings, sultans, the Shah. Photos, framed notes, and other documents told the story of the American century. I thought, "Hey, this job's going to be all right!"

To raise money for the NPR Foundation, we invited donors to watch us produce a radio program—in the East Room of the White House during the Clinton administration. Produced by our in-house impresario Murray Horwitz, vice president for cultural programming, the show included a performance of *1776*, a play by A. E. Hotchner, who was present. Linda Wertheimer, Carl Kasell, Tom and Ray Magliozzi, Martin Goldsmith, and I were "supported" by this cast: Martin Sheen, Edward James Olmos, Kathleen Turner, Jason Robards, Lolita Davidovich, Roscoe Lee Brown, Blythe Danner, and Robert Klein. Also on the bill were Bette Midler, Taj Mahal, and Michael Weinstein. Afterwards, there were drinks and a buffet with Bill and Hill.

For those who don't believe a journalist should sip bourbon with an elected official, I remind you that this was a fund-raiser for NPR, not for Bill Clinton. Besides, it's a Washington custom to accept the invitation of any president as long as no journalistic principle is compromised. One goes out of respect for the office, not the man. That's *our* house he's living in; we only let him use it for a while.

Seeing the less regal America is rewarding in other ways. My travels for NPR took me to Appalachia, a region where geography, politics, and absentee corporate landowners have denied the people a viable economic base, resulting in poverty, mediocre education, and poor health care. When I saw Appalachia, I thought I had seen the worst of what happens when people can't control their own fate. I had not yet seen the Indian reservations of South Dakota.

My visits to the Pine Ridge and Rosebud Sioux reservations were inspired by writer Michael Dorris. Reading my hometown paper one day, I saw a feature story about Michael and his first novel. I remembered him from high school. We were not friends at St. X because he was two years ahead of me and was one of the scholars, not the jocks. After reading his novel, I interviewed him, and our friendship was under way. I soon learned that Michael, whose father was descended from the Modoc tribe, had adopted three Indian children. As each of the children reached toddler stage, problems became apparent, especially with Abel, the eldest. Michael investigated and learned that each of his children had been born to an alcoholic mother who drank heavily during pregnancy. The children's prenatal diet had been mostly alcohol. Abel had permanent brain damage, the result of Fetal Alcohol Syndrome (FAS). The other two children had the less obvious symptoms of Fetal Alcohol Effect (FAE). *The Broken Cord*, Michael's book about all this, is the definitive layperson's work on the subject.

It was a heartbreaking story, and I wanted to do more than the standard book interview with Michael. I interviewed doctors, medical researchers, and recovering alcoholic mothers who had borne FAS children, and I went to the reservations where alcoholism and its effects are major problems. NPR's Margaret Low Smith, Barry Gordemer, and Dennis Nielsen were with me in South Dakota, and what we saw there has left a lasting impression on all of us. Alcohol is not sold on the reservations, but it's available in quantity at stores in a Nebraska town that borders Pine Ridge. On the day the government checks arrive, those stores are jammed with people who have no jobs, no hope, or no sense. I had known alcoholics all my life, but I had never seen anyone buy a case of beer, walk to a nearby shade tree, sit down, and drink until passing out or exhausting the supply. People were literally drinking themselves to death. Others were killed by drunk drivers who didn't see them trying to stagger home. Counselors told of women, their judgment (or defenses) impaired by alcohol, giving birth to FAS children who would never have a chance. Our five-part series was titled "Born Drunk," and it won a Gabriel Award.

I've been to happier places, traveling to all fifty states on behalf of NPR, meeting listeners and hearing stories. I have thrown the first pitch at four major-league baseball stadiums (St. Louis, Detroit, San Francisco, and Cincinnati) and one minor-league park (Grand Rapids). The owners of all other teams should be advised that the home team has won every game at which I've pitched.

I had a different role in 1997 at Turner Field in Atlanta when the Braves celebrated the fiftieth anniversary of Jackie Robinson's integrating major league baseball. The ceremonial pitcher that night was retired General Colin Powell. My job was to be the master of ceremonies for the pregame program, which included the very old and infirm vibraphonist Lionel Hampton. Hampton was in midtune when he fell backward onto the field. No one moved to help this great legend of jazz—so *I* did. He had not dropped his hammers, so when I stood him up he just resumed playing the vibes as if nothing had happened. The bass player leaned toward my ear and said, "Stay where you are." Good advice, because once more Hamp listed back toward me, and I nudged him forward again. The Braves chartered a Lear jet to fly Powell and me to Atlanta. My daughter Susannah came along too, as well as Powell's son, Michael, and a grandson. During the game, we were seated in Ted Turner's box (Turner wasn't there), and Michael Powell made a splendid bare-handed grab of a one-hop foul ball. Good hands for a communications lawyer who later would become perhaps the worst-ever chairman of the Federal Communications Commission.

NPR gave me tons of memories, and I remain grateful for them.

WAR

━━━━━

For forty years, Harry Belafonte had been trying to get his recording project on the market. It was the history of African American music in the New World and titled *The Long Road to Freedom*. He'd been at it so long that the technology of music recording had changed, and now the eighty songs would be on five compact discs, packaged with a hardback book and a bonus DVD. I was in my office reviewing all this material in preparation for my first interview with one of America's musical legends.

Outside my door, half a dozen members of the *Morning Edition* staff were watching television. A plane had struck one of the towers of the World Trade Center. No one was talking about a commercial airliner, so it was assumed to be a single-engine aircraft that probably had mechanical failure, since the weather in New York was beautiful. A local story but worthy of mention in a newscast. I joined the little TV audience for a minute or so, and we saw a second plane enter the picture and crash into the WTC's other tower. It was clearly *not* a local story, and Harry Belafonte would have to be interviewed some other day.

I anchored live, unscripted radio for the next four hours until another crew took over for the *Morning Edition* unit. On that horrifying day, many Americans asked what they could do; we were among the lucky ones who knew what we could do—we could do our jobs. I still get compliments from people who heard us. They always say we were so calm and that they appreciated that. I think some of it had to do with our being radio. The video images were so powerful, so vivid, and so dramatic that TV couldn't resist showing them again and again. We had only the pictures we made with our words, and those pictures were not so devastating. Interviews with ordinary New Yorkers helped us paint some of the pictures, and they were enormously good at it. This was the day I learned that anyone with a cell phone is a potential reporter.

Two political careers were revived by the attacks on New York and Washington. Mayor Rudy Giuliani had been ridiculed by the New York press for the messes he'd made of both his political career and his personal life. Praise for his performance on 9/11 gave him notions of running for president. As for the man who was holding that job, he had no real standing until al-Qaeda's attack. George W. Bush was the loser of the popular vote for president in 2000. He owed his election "victory" to a five-to-four partisan vote of the Supreme Court, which had earlier halted the recount of votes in Florida. The president wasted much of September 11 aboard Air Force One, flying all over the United States while his aides tried to figure out what to do next. Ultimately, he made his way to Ground Zero, stood atop a pile of rubble, hugged a firefighter, and looked presidential. His ratings soared to 80-something percent, and he had the nation ready to follow him to war against terrorists in Afghanistan. Bring it on! Let's roll. Even Neil Young was on board. The nation was a sea of American flags.

We know now that neoconservatives high in the Bush administration had already been pushing for U.S. military action in Iraq. The attacks by al-Qaeda on New York and Washington presented opportunity for the neocons to tuck their pet cause into the War on Terror. Even before the battle of Tora Bora, when Osama bin Laden slipped away and the Taliban were driven into Pakistan to regroup and fight another day, we were hearing of a connection to Saddam Hussein in Iraq. (Never mind that Saddam saw al-Qaeda as a threat and would not allow bin Laden into his country.) All that was needed to extend the war to Iraq was a clever campaign to dupe the media into believing such a connection actually existed.

It was a brilliant strategy—so simple, yet so effective. As the United States prepared for the first anniversary of 9/11, prominent Iraqi exiles told the *New York Times* that Saddam was well on his way to developing a nuclear bomb. That was followed up by having "Bush administration officials" confirm the story and be the official sources cited in the lead of the *Times* story. Then, on the day the *Times* story appeared—Sunday, September 8, 2002—prominent Bush administration officials were dispatched to the Sunday interview shows to lend some "credibility" to the *Times* story. That was the day national security adviser Condoleezza Rice told Wolf Blitzer on CNN that Saddam was only six months away from having the bomb and that "we don't want the smoking gun to be a mushroom cloud." Meanwhile, over on NBC's *Meet the Press*, Vice President Dick Cheney was having a problem. He was now many minutes into the program, and Tim Russert had not cited that morning's story in the *New York Times*. So, awkwardly, Cheney had to bring it up himself: "There's a story in the *New York Times* this morning—this is—I don't—and I want to attribute the *Times*. I don't want to talk about, obviously, specific intelligence sources, but it's now public that, in fact, he has been seeking to acquire, and we have been able to intercept and prevent him from acquiring through this particular channel, the kinds of tubes that are necessary to build a centrifuge."

Well no wonder he didn't want to talk about specific intelligence sources! It would expose his Iraqi exiles as administration tools. But the most important words in that statement were "it's now public." It was "now public" because Cheney, Rice, and others made sure it was public, and it was all crap. Saddam had no bomb. The Bush administration lied to American citizens to get them to support an invasion of Iraq. It worked brilliantly. Years into the war, an astonishing percentage of Americans still connected Saddam Hussein to 9/11.

As everyone now knows, most of the media rolled over. The editorial pages of the *Washington Post* and the *New York Times* enthusiastically endorsed the invasion of Iraq. TV reporters sporting their flag lapel pins beat the drums of war. There were exceptions. At the *New Yorker*, Seymour Hersh was helping Pentagon generals vent their hatred of defense secretary Donald Rumsfeld. At the *Washington Post*, Walter Pincus was asking his estimable intelligence sources if any of this "weapons of mass destruction" talk was true, and they told him no. Pincus's knockdowns of *Post* headline stories were buried on page 16. And the superheroes of the moment were Warren Strobel and Jonathan Landay, who were reporters in the Washington bureau of the Knight-Ridder newspapers—a chain that no longer exists. The K-R reporters questioned the WMD stories and the nonexistent links between 9/11 and Saddam. The problem for Knight-Ridder was that the chain had no newspapers in New York or Washington. Most of the country's movers and shakers never read the K-R stories.

The Bush administration wanted no dissent. If you weren't with them, you were against them and you supported terrorism. Georgia senator Max Cleland, who voted to authorize the invasion of Iraq, lost his 2002 reelection bid because he supported a homeland security bill that differed from the president's. Voters did not mind the audacity of national leaders who dodged service in Vietnam questioning the patriotism of Cleland, who lost three of his limbs there. On ABC's *Politically Incorrect*, Bill Maher questioned the characterization of the 9/11 attackers as cowards and lost his sponsors (and ultimately his program). White House news secretary Ari Fleischer said Maher's comments were "reminders to all Americans that they need to watch what they say, watch what they do. This is not a time for remarks like that." Politically incorrect indeed!

White House management of news and opinion reached a ridiculous extreme on the night of March 6, 2003, when President Bush held a news conference. Although he'd been in office more than two years, this was only his eighth news conference and just his second in prime time—but this one was extraordinary for other reasons. Members of the White House press corps did not just file into the room; they were summoned in pairs and ushered into the East Room two-by-two, like animals boarding Noah's Ark. CBS reporter Bill Plante said it was "as if we were in grammar school and were being called on the line for something." Reporters were assigned seats corresponding to a chart prepared for President Bush by news secretary Fleischer. The president used the chart to choose which reporters to recognize. Among those passed over were reporters from *TIME*, *Newsweek*, the *Washington Post*, *USA Today*, and NPR. The TV regulars made the cut, however, and there was an interesting moment when CNN's John King attempted to ask a question. The president stopped him and said, "This is scripted," then called the next name on his list—John King.

I felt the questions the president was asked that night were lame—especially since everyone in the East Room knew the United States was about to invade Iraq. The Bush administration had successfully manipulated the White House press corps at a time when pointed inquiries were needed the most. I decided to make this outrage a big part of the speech I was scheduled to make at the University of Kentucky in Lexington.

On April 8, 2003, I was among those inducted that year into the Kentucky Journalism Hall of Fame. On the same day, I had the honor of delivering the annual Joe Creason Lecture, which is a part of the induction activities. I concede that I had reservations about being so bold that day. When people pay you high tribute, you're tempted to say the sorts of things that won't upset the people who are being so nice to you—just smile, be humble, and leave everyone happy. If I questioned the then-prevailing national group-speak of blind compliance with the push to a wider war, people would inevitably see it as an anti-Bush speech. People would likely miss my point about the importance of asking tough questions and then, if one were so moved, to feel free to dissent. In April 2003, such a speech would only be seen as anti-Bush, especially in red state Kentucky, where the governor, both senators, and five of six representatives were Republican. What kind of reception would I get in the state that's home to Fort Knox and Fort Campbell?

On the other hand, I was being inducted into the Kentucky Journalism Hall of Fame. How could I accept that honor and then deliver some lame, feel-good homily? Plus, I felt a duty to deliver a Joe Creason Lecture worthy of Joe Creason, whose column was a must-read feature of the Louisville *Courier-Journal* when I was growing up. Joe wouldn't have wanted me to pull my punches. So I let 'er rip.

I began by lamenting that most of Kentucky's newspapers and its radio and TV stations were no longer home-owned, as they were when I lived there from 1947 through 1969. Then I went into the sorry state of media consolidation, which was choking the spectrum of public opinion—the number of voices and viewpoints was ever-shrinking. I railed against Clear Channel for owning 1,250 of the country's 10,000 radio stations and against the FCC, under then-chairman Michael Powell (Colin's son), for wanting even fewer companies to own still more stations. I pointed out that the anti-Bush Dixie Chicks needed to be heard on the radio if they were going to make a living, but a lot of country stations controlled by these huge conglomerates objected to the Chicks' politics and didn't want to play their records—echoes of the blacklisting era. Then I cited a *Washington Post* story of the previous week and said this to the audience:

> A Cleveland company called McVay Media describes itself as the largest radio consulting firm in the world. McVay developed a memo to its client stations advising them on how to use the war to their best business advantage. Called a "War Manual, the memo says the stations should "Get the following production pieces into the studio NOW . . . patriotic music that makes you cry, salute, get cold chills! Go for the emotion. . . . Air the National Anthem at a specified time each day as long as the USA is at war." The article also quotes Michael Harrison, publisher of *Talkers*, a journal for the radio talk business. Harrison says, "It's counterintuitive for hosts and program directors to pay too much attention to the antiwar movement right now."

That same *Post* article mentioned advice from the TV news consulting firm Frank N. Magid Associates: "Covering war protests may be harmful to a station's bottom line." Andrew Jay Schwartzman of the Media Access Project linked all of this back to the tide of media consolidation, saying, "With increasing concentration of ownership, if one or two big companies are using the same corporate-wide policy, or relying on the same consultants, there aren't enough competitive forces" to ensure alternative opinions.

Continuing my lecture, I went into President Bush's news conference of the month before and proposed a list of questions that I wished had been asked. I'll admit my "questions" were a bit smart-alecky, but I wanted my speech to be both entertaining and provocative—so I was going for laughs. For example, given that Britain's prime minister Tony

Blair was taking heat for supporting war in Iraq, I suggested this as a question for President Bush: Is it possible the war in Iraq will result in regime change in Great Britain? Here are four more:

> When I interviewed your wife, Mr. President, she said the best by-product of ousting the Taliban from Afghanistan was the liberation of Afghan women. Defense secretary Donald Rumsfeld told me the same thing when I asked him what the U.S. had achieved in its war in Afghanistan. If the liberation of Arab women is so important to your administration, then why is the United States not invading Saudi Arabia?
>
> You offered an attractive bribe to Turkey in exchange for permission to use Turkey as a base from which to invade northern Iraq. Was the vote of the Turkish parliament to refuse the offer an example of the democracy you're trying to establish in the Middle East?
>
> Mr. President, you've spent billions of dollars on homeland security only to see the nation's capital paralyzed by a North Carolina tobacco farmer driving his tractor onto the Mall. Did homeland security secretary Tom Ridge miss a memo or two?
>
> Sir, would you say your policy of noninvolvement in the Israeli-Palestinian conflict is working out? If so, for whom?

There were others just as snarky, and all in the spirit of conservative columnist George Will, who does this sort of presentation frequently.

The response to the speech in the hall that night was very warm. David Hawpe of the Louisville *Courier-Journal* was enthusiastic about it and kept it on his paper's website for quite some time. Unfortunately, a student journalist gave it a different spin that was picked up by a few papers. Bruce Drake, NPR's vice president for news, asked me if that account was accurate. I told him no and gave him the proper context. I never heard another word from him or anyone else at NPR. Were the NPR suits upset about what I'd said in Lexington? I had no idea.

There was not a lot of national attention paid to my remarks except for the Clear Channel stations, which roughed me up a bit. Most disappointing was an attack by the company's major voice in Louisville, my hometown. This guy went to my high school, yet his reaction to my speech was a total suck-up to his employer.

Exactly one year later, in April 2004, Bill Moyers and a camera crew from the PBS program *Now* interviewed me at NPR about my recent firing from *Morning Edition*. Right off the bat, Bill brought up my speech in Lexington and asked if that was why I'd lost my program. I was stunned. I hadn't thought about that year-old speech in quite a while. Now this question had brought it back—plus Drake's email about the account by the student journalist. Mulling over all of this, I told Bill that I just didn't know. I honestly didn't know why I'd been canned. Years later, as I write these words, I still don't know.

TWO BABES IN BAGHDAD

———

I remain in awe of my NPR colleagues who reported the wars. They have been under fire, have been held prisoner by ugly regimes, and have endured the worst hardships. Anne Garrels is one of them.

As war with Iraq became inevitable, major American news organizations pulled their reporters out of Iraq. Annie stayed, and she was one of the very few who did. She and I had a daily on-air conversation as the United States prepared to bomb Baghdad—where Annie was. She was living in the Palestine Hotel, a place where British journalists would later be killed by U.S. troops who didn't like reporters looking at them through binoculars. Anne was in the hotel that day.

Back in this preinvasion period, Annie would give me daily descriptions of the U.S. bombing campaign, speaking to me on a satellite telephone she was not supposed to have, equipment she kept hidden until the moment came when she had to send her reports to NPR. What I didn't know at the time is that one of us was not wearing clothes. Annie's memoir of this period is titled *Naked in Baghdad*. She had this idea that if the authorities knocked on her door, the Muslim men would allow her to get dressed before they entered. This would give her time to return the illegal sat phone to its hiding place and throw on a dress she had laid out for the occasion.

I knew nothing of this until she came out with her book. It is entirely sexist and unprofessional of me to say that Annie is someone you wouldn't mind seeing naked—but I think it adds a lot to this story to know that. So my first reaction to *Naked in Baghdad* was regret that I never once asked her in those on-air conversations, "So Annie, what are you wearing?"

One of those talks took the air out of my lungs. That was the morning she told me that Saddam's thugs took five journalists prisoner and one of those in custody was photojournalist Molly Bingham. Molly is a friend of mine from Louisville, where her family ran the *Courier-Journal* newspaper and other media properties for most of the twentieth century. I knew that Molly's father, former C-J editor Barry Bingham, Jr., was one of my regular listeners. Sure enough, that's how he heard that his younger daughter was Saddam's prisoner. Molly spent eight days at Abu Ghraib prison at a time before Saddam's torturers gave way to America's. Molly wasn't tortured in a physical way, but it was a shocking episode for a young journalist who speaks frankly of her privileged background. Just months later, she was back in Baghdad, reporting on the American occupation for *Vanity Fair*. Then she and another photojournalist, Steve Connors, collaborated on a documentary film called *Meeting Resistance*. Most of what I know of the Iraqi resistance to the American occupation is what I learned from Molly and Steve's interviews with the insurgents. Not many other American journalists bothered to get their side of the story.

TURNING POINT

—

In late October 2002, I received a letter from Hana Lane, senior editor at the John Wiley & Sons publishing house. She invited me to become one of the authors for a new series of volumes Wiley called Turning Points. "In the spirit of the 'Penguin Lives' series of short biographies," Hana wrote, "these books are capsule histories on significant moments." Other authors in the series included Alan Dershowitz, Eleanor Clift, Douglas Brinkley, William F. Buckley, Jr., William Least Heat Moon, Sir Martin Gilbert, Thomas Fleming, and my public radio colleagues Scott Simon and Martin Goldsmith. Seemed like good company to me, so I agreed. I asked if I could write about Edward R. Murrow, who had been the force behind two turning points—the establishment of radio as a source of original journalism in 1938 and the establishment of television as a source of original journalism in 1951. Wiley agreed to that, and we had a book deal. It was perfect for me. Wiley wanted fewer than two hundred pages, and the focus would be narrow—Murrow as broadcast journalism pioneer, not his whole life. I could easily write this book in afternoons and on weekends and not have to take a leave of absence. So that's how I spent my spare time throughout 2003—writing my Murrow book to be published in 2004.

Andy Danyo of NPR's corporate communications department was excited about the book because it would give her a tool for promoting me. A classics major when she was at the University of Georgia, Andy is very smart and has an endearing Gracie Allen gift for malaprops that really aren't. We were once discussing how I'd be received at a station I was about to visit. She told me, "Your reputation exceeds you," which is absolutely true. Andy had been a lobbyist for growers of peanuts and Vidalia onions before joining the staff of Georgia senator Max Cleland, for whom she occasionally wrote speeches. Andy had always wanted to work for NPR, so she took the first available opening—doing public relations for NPR programs and the people who made them. One of her jobs was to coordinate travel for hosts and reporters visiting NPR's member stations. She was enormously efficient at this and made those trips a pleasure for me. We became good pals because I was one of the few NPR newsies who liked to visit stations. Most of the others considered it an onerous chore and would turn down station requests. Andy didn't like begging NPR people to do promotional work, nor did she like disappointing stations.

Andy and I started plotting out the promotional prospects for 2004. In February, I would celebrate my thirtieth anniversary at NPR. The book would come out in May, and I would do a modest tour that would include stops at stations. The book would be a great premium when stations held their fall fund-raisers. Finally, on November 5, we'd have the glorious silver anniversary of *Morning Edition*. It would be a stellar year for engaging the public and telling *Morning Edition*'s story. Those were our plans. Alas, NPR had made other plans.

My thirtieth anniversary should have given me a clue. There was no public hoopla at all and precious little notice in-house. There was cake and orange juice. Yippee! I have to be the only thirty-year employee who never received a gift from NPR. Company president Kevin Klose paid a rare visit to the *Morning Edition* area to have some cake with the guy he had decided to fire.

On March 9, I got an email from Andy notifying me of a late-morning meeting concerning the upcoming book tour. It was a lie. Andy and her entire department had already been told that I was getting canned that day. Andy knew that my meeting did not involve a book tour and that she would not be there. The suits used Andy to lure me to my firing.

The meeting was held in the office of Jay Kernis, the senior vice president for programming, a man who produced audio promos for me thirty years earlier, one of my oldest and dearest friends at NPR. Also there was the vice president for news, Bruce Drake, who did not say one word at any time during the proceedings. The only other participant was Ken Greene, a representative of my union, AFTRA, the American Federation of Television and Radio Artists. As Kernis often does, he read from a script. "We're making a change," he began. Continuing his reading, Kernis said my last *Morning Edition* program would be on Friday, April 30. I did the math and realized that would be precisely twenty-four-and-a-half years since the debut broadcast. I said, "But what about the twenty-fifth anniversary in November?" Kernis replied, "The anniversary will be about the future, not about the past." He said I was to become a senior correspondent (the same fate as previously demoted hosts) and that he didn't care if I only filed reports three times a year. The details of my arrangement were to be worked out with the company through AFTRA's Ken Greene, and I was to keep quiet about all this until March 22. He didn't say thanks for thirty years of dedicated service to the company—thanks for making *Morning Edition* the most listened-to program in the history of public radio—thanks for raising all that money for member stations—thanks for the twenty thousand interviews—there was a lot he didn't say.

I went back to my office, called Sharon, and told her, "Well, you can have a dog." She knew that meant I was leaving *Morning Edition*. We once had a dog who barked when I tried to nap. When that dog went to her reward, she was not replaced. There'd be no need for naps anymore, so a dog was back in the picture.

Next I called Andy, who feigned surprise. Only much, much later would she come clean about knowing before I did.

I wrote a statement for the March 22 announcement saying I was still going to be on the air, thanking listeners for their support, and urging them to continue supporting their local stations. On March 16, I took the letter to the office of Jess Sarmiento, the communications director of public and media relations. As I left her office, Jay Kernis walked in. Here's what happened next—as told to me in an email by Andy, whose desk was just outside Sarmiento's door:

> He came in and said, "Tell me everything. Was he horrible?" Jess said it
> was a great meeting and that you had come up with your own statement

that was near perfection. Jay started reading it, mimicking you in a really obnoxious way. I think even editing as he went. It was really obnoxious. And then he looked at me and said, "I understand you're not a fan of this decision." And when I started to respond, he interrupted, "I just want you to know that I'm not enjoying this. Wait, I take that back. I am enjoying every second."

Firings are messy and some people react in a most hostile fashion. NPR employees once received a memo titled "A Person of Interest." The memo concerned a recently fired person who was now stalking NPR. He had been spotted urinating on a bench out in front of the building. "Person of Interest?" It was a curious way to refer to someone, and we all had fun with the phrase. So when I made my announcement to the *Morning Edition* staff on March 22, I joked that there were three stages in my NPR career—host, senior correspondent, and person of interest— and that I had reached stage two. Several of my colleagues were in tears, but others were relieved. They figured I had called them together to announce I was leaving to undergo cancer treatment. Oh, he's just fired.

This was the same day NPR issued a press release saying I was leaving the host job to become a senior correspondent. When they showed me the release in advance, I told them not to put it out. I had not agreed to become a senior correspondent because the promised negotiations between NPR and Ken Greene had not taken place. There would be no such agreement until I knew the terms and conditions of my new situation. I was especially interested in what they were going to pay me. The demotion was insulting enough; I sure wasn't going to take an additional hit in the wallet. NPR paid no attention to me and put out the release anyway. That was a big mistake. The press called me and asked if I had agreed to the demotion and I said no. That's when it hit the fan.

When I was a management major at the University of Louisville, my textbooks were loaded with case studies we'd review and then have to say what the company did wrong and how it might have executed better. My ouster was a classic case study in bungling a firing.

First of all, many NPR managers never understood radio. Its leaders have come from education or government or newspapers. They've never been at microphones communicating with an audience, and they don't understand the bond that is formed as a result. For thirty years, NPR listeners welcomed me into their cars, their homes, their bedrooms—even their bathrooms, with the invention of the shower radio. This radio stuff gets intimate! They took me with them on business trips and vacations. When they moved to new towns, they found I was already waiting there for them when they arrived and they took comfort in that—something important in their lives had not changed despite the move. Mine was the voice that woke them up for many years, the one they were accustomed to, the one that told them everything was all right and they could safely start another day. To NPR management, people and jobs are interchangeable: you have a slot and you have a person—you fill the slot with the person and you move on. Sorry, that's not how a loyal audience regards its radio buddy.

Andy Danyo says Jay Kernis told her department to expect 400 letters from listeners protesting my firing. Instead, they got 50,000 emails and hundreds of letters, many of them saying, "If it ain't broke, don't fix it," and comparing NPR's decision to the flap over "New Coke." NPR had to hire six temps at sixteen dollars an hour to deal with the volume—so I was good for the economy. In addition, an online petition demanding that NPR reverse its decision was launched by Edward Chapman, a freshman at George Washington University. Who says I don't appeal to the young demographic? Chapman, who is well on his way to achieving his career goal of becoming a political operative on the scale of Karl Rove and James Carville, collected more than 26,000 signers before he hit Print and brought the petition over to me in a big box. I can't wait to interview him someday when he's managing a presidential race.

The press hammered NPR. It was front-page news in the *Washington Post*, which also carried an editorial, as did the *Chicago Tribune*. The arts and entertainment sections of the other major papers played the story prominently. There were columns and op-eds by Linda Ellerbee, David Broder, Ellen Goodman, Richard Cohen, Marc Fisher, and many others. I initiated none of this, speaking only when spoken to.

Representative David Dreier (R-CA) spoke on my behalf on the floor of the House of Representatives. Senator Tom Harkin (D-IA) blasted NPR executives by name and declared I deserved a raise, not removal. Senator Dick Durbin (D-IL) made two speeches in the Senate. In one, he suspected I might have been the victim of age discrimination, and he said, "This decision by National Public Radio is the wrong decision. If it is the marketing belief of NPR that they need to have a fresh voice, they are missing the big picture." Both Harkin and Durbin urged the public to send protest emails to NPR.

After I interviewed Senator Ernest "Fritz" Hollings (D-SC), the senator told me, "And don't let them put you aside."

The most amazing reaction to my situation was passed on to me by reporter Nancy Solomon, who was covering the Tyco trial, then very big in the news. In the courtroom, Mark Swartz, one of two codefendants accused of looting millions from Tyco, said to Nancy, "How can they do this to Bob just six months before the twenty-fifth anniversary?" A guy facing twenty years for grand larceny is concerned about *my* fate?

Listener protests and a bad press were not NPR's biggest problems. NPR chose to fire me when its member stations were in the middle of their spring fund-raising campaigns. The great thing about public radio is that listeners actually pay the bills—their contributions make up the bulk of each station's operating budget. You do *not* want to anger them when you're begging them to write you a check. NPR made listeners angry, and they took it out on the totally innocent stations, which had nothing to do with my firing. Imagine the calls that station managers made to NPR executives when listeners said they weren't going to support the station anymore. Through multiple channels, I made a number of appeals to listeners to continue supporting their local stations, which were now victims as much as I was.

Listeners demanded an explanation of my dismissal—my "reassignment," as NPR was calling it. The company's press release stated that I was being replaced in order to "refresh the program to meet the changing needs of listeners." Listeners had not discerned that their needs had changed, and they recognized press-release gobbledygook when they saw it. When Ken Stern, the company's chief operating officer, declared it was "part of the natural evolution of the program," emailers mocked him with numerous simian metaphors. This was a crowd that knew all about evolution.

The protest swelled, and NPR decided Jay Kernis would have an online chat with listeners. Kernis answered questions selected by NPR ombudsman Jeffrey Dvorkin and his assistant, Ariana Pekary (who, like Andy, is now an award-winning producer of *The Bob Edwards Show*). Over his shoulder, Jeffrey was getting helpful advice from Ken Stern, who kept pointing to the screen and shouting, "Take *that* one—take *that* one," until Jeffrey said, "Fuck off, Ken."

NPR tried again, telling the *Los Angeles Times* that I was fired because I didn't want to have a cohost. I didn't, but I was not asked to accept one, nor was I told that one would be imposed on me. If management had told me I was to have a cohost, I'd still be doing the program today. It turned out that they *did* want cohosts, but they didn't want me to be one of them; they wanted me gone.

Still looking for cover, NPR blamed the stations. Kernis planted a story in the *New York Times* on March 30 saying stations wanted changes at NPR and that he decided I was the change they needed. This directly contradicted a Q&A sheet that NPR sent to stations on March 22. One of the questions was: "Have member stations asked NPR to make this change in *Morning Edition*?" "No." The next question: "Was this decision by you or in conjunction with member stations?" Answer: "This change was the decision of NPR Programming and News management." Now eight days later, NPR tells the *Times* something different.

The *Times* story was very odd in that it quoted only four people from the stations and three of them were supportive of me. The fourth one said, "It is time for evolutionary change." There's that evolution thing again—right from the Kernis/Stern hymnal. Kernis raised questions about my worth as a reporter—a ridiculous thing to do, considering he had just made me a reporter. He also said this all went back to the network's slow response to the 9/11 attacks, implying that this had something to do with me. This was a contemptible slander, because decisions about when and how to cover stories were made by Jay Kernis, Bruce Drake, and the many editors and producers at NPR news. I broke in to *Morning Edition* when they told me to do it at about 9:20 AM, and I didn't let up until I was relieved at 1 PM. If NPR feels bad about our 9/11 coverage, it should return the Peabody Award we won for it.

Actor Henry Winkler called me that day to try to cheer me up. So did Garrison Keillor, who recognized the *Times* story for exactly what it was. He said, "Don't hit that tar baby." He was counseling me to ignore the bait and stay on the high road.

When I arrived home that day, Sharon handed me one of those FedEx cardboard envelopes. I ripped it open and read a proposition from Hugh Panero, the CEO of XM Satellite Radio. He wanted me to do a daily, one-hour interview program called *The Bob Edwards Show*. He had it all laid out—a signing bonus, a salary, and stock options. The clincher was this line: "Maybe Jay Kernis doesn't want to hear you every day, but I do." That was exactly what I needed to read on the worst day of my life, so I said yes.

I still had a month of *Morning Edition* programs to do and made certain I went out with some great interviews. On my last show, on April 30, 2004, the very last interview was with Charles Osgood, my morning rival on CBS for my whole *Morning Edition* run. This was partly symbolic because Charlie was the *first* person I interviewed on the program twenty-four-and-a-half years earlier. Among his considerable talents is a gift for doggerel. He's often done his entire show in doggerel—on deadline! I treasure one he wrote for me in 1999:

> Every morning it makes me smile
> To know folks are hearing *The Osgood File*.
> But some folks are not—I have competition
> From Bob Edwards and his great show, *Morning Edition*.
> We're both on at the same time and therefore you see,
> I can't listen to him—he can't listen to me.
> But nevertheless, I admire him plenty.
> Congratulations Bob Edwards on year number 20.

I made a little speech at the end of that last show, thanking listeners, member stations and their staffs, my family, and the hundreds of *Morning Edition* staff members over those many years. Then I said goodbye. Apparently that was not the speech management was expecting, because two of my superiors were in the control room for the entire show expecting me to have a moment like the fictional Howard Beale had in the movie *Network*. Since they had never attended my broadcast before, I'm sure they were there to silence my microphone if I went into some bridge-burning rant. It says volumes about NPR managers at the time that they had no clue about my character and professionalism. That they would think I'd trash all those years of on-air goodwill is testimony to how little they knew about their anchor.

On that same day, Oregon's *Portland Tribune* carried a story in which NPR president Kevin Klose said that I was offered a chance to cohost my show: "That was the idea—to work it out and find the right person" [to anchor with him], Klose said. "But he turned it down." Absolutely not true. Klose needed *something* to explain my firing to donors, the stations, and his board. The cohost fiction is what he chose. Later, I managed to get NPR to issue an official statement saying it never asked me to be a cohost of my program.

MAVERICK

———

Should I have seen it coming—that truck that hit me on March 9, 2004?

I was a company man who loved NPR, but I was never a contender for employee of the month (not that NPR has such a thing). People in the news business disagree about the value of stories and how they should be covered—and these disagreements can sometimes be spirited, even passionate. I think it's a healthy thing that makes a news organization stronger. Maybe over the course of thirty years, a company gets tired of hearing it and fires the guy who won't immediately salute.

The time I thought I might get the axe was back in 1996 when Bill Buzenberg was the vice president for news. Bill had ambitious plans for expanding NPR's news coverage but lacked the reporting staff to do the job. Management wouldn't authorize the hiring of more staff reporters, so Bill developed a nationwide team of twenty stringers under contract and on retainer to report for NPR. This was all very good for our network but not from my union perspective. Bill had established a shadow team of nonunion freelancers whose first reporting responsibilities were to NPR, but they were not getting NPR pay and benefits. Some were being compensated at about a third of what staff reporters were making. In the event of a strike, workers belonging to AFTRA would be out on the street while these twenty stringers would be turning out *Morning Edition* and *All Things Considered*. AFTRA was fighting to get these reporters covered by the union contract, so it threatened to take

NPR to the Internal Revenue Service and the National Labor Relations Board and also to tell our story to the *Washington Post*. Bill Buzenberg noticed that when I introduced any of the twenty on the air, I never said "NPR's so-and-so reports," merely "so-and-so reports." He insisted I say "NPR's" because they were on retainer and under contract to the network. I replied that the only contract I was under was the AFTRA contract and I didn't want to violate it by identifying nonunion reporters as "NPR's." He said, "Well, if it's a union issue, get the union in here and we'll straighten this out." So I did. AFTRA's Ken Greene met with NPR management, and ultimately all the contract reporters were put on staff. The happiest person about all of this was Bill Buzenberg, whose reporting staff had just been expanded by twenty people covering cities from Raleigh to San Francisco. It was actually twenty-two reporters because Bill threw in a couple of temps. (NPR also had contract reporters back in 1982 and agreed to hire them once AFTRA took the network to the NLRB. That's how Jacki Lyden and Howard Berkes joined the staff.)

I gave Bill fits, but I didn't mean to. I liked him a lot and I still do, but we clashed on even trivial matters. He didn't like the way I said the word "harassment" on the air. I say *hare*-ass-ment with the emphasis on the first syllable. He hated that because everyone else said it differently, and he insisted that I be like everyone else. I tried to joke with him about it and said he was trying to put the ass back into harassment. I hoped he'd smile if I said he was harassing me. He didn't.

That piece of silliness illustrates another problem I had with my company. The freewheeling, experimental atmosphere of NPR evaporated once the place grew big, important, and popular with the public. The bureaucracy mushroomed with executives, producers, and editors. It became a top-down kind of place where authority was asserted and conformity demanded. The number of NPR employees who could call *Morning Edition* and order a change in my introduction to a story seemed infinite. There were too many bosses to please. Micromanagement is no fun—probably not even for the micromanager. Hosts and reporters should not be reprimanded for quirks and idiosyncrasies that distinguish them from the standard-issue radio personality, as long as what they're doing doesn't color the story or alter the facts. Long ago, there used to be a *Morning Edition* way of covering a story that differed from the *All Things Considered* style of reporting. That was stamped out in favor of the central office NPR "brand" identity. I have to acknowledge that the NPR brass were hugely successful in selling the NPR "brand," but I think they could have accomplished this while still preserving the individual identities of the programs and the people who hosted those programs. There was no need to impose vanilla on us. I believe we could have been just as successful—or perhaps more so—while tolerating some variety.

The rise of the cable news channels dramatically altered NPR's news priorities. CNN had the field to itself until FOX News and MSNBC came along. In the intense rivalry that ensued, each of the channels made coverage of live events a big priority. If FOX went to a live but marginally important event somewhere, it would flash the words "Breaking News" on the screen and have it blink on and off to get your attention. If all went the way FOX hoped, CNN would look lame by comparison because it wasn't on this "Breaking News" story. Naturally, CNN responded to this tactic by aping it, and then all three cable news channels were switching to "Breaking News" stories that might consist of nothing more than President Bush walking to his helicopter or maybe one of those aerial views of a freeway chase by the LAPD. Gradually this nonsense took over at NPR. As I heard the story, the managers of NPR stations would call our executives and ask why *Morning Edition* wasn't covering the "Breaking News" story the managers were watching on CNN. Sure enough, I'd be sent into the studio for an "update" of the second or third feed of *Morning Edition*. This "update" would replace a piece of real journalism that had run in the program's first feed. Instead of hearing a well-crafted piece of reporting that might have been weeks in the making, listeners would hear me talking live with White House reporter Don Gonyea concerning what the president might be about to say in the Rose Garden. Sometimes there'd be actual news, sometimes not—but it was seldom anything worth more than a mention in the newscast at the top of the hour. I felt NPR should exercise its own news judgment and not have it determined by a competitive situation among cable TV channels. NPR believed its competition was CNN—I believed it was the *New York Times*.

When NPR began in 1970, program director Bill Siemering wrote a stirring network mission statement that included this: "In its journalistic mode, National Public Radio will actively explore, investigate and interpret issues of national and international import. The programs will enable the individual to better understand himself, his government, his institutions and his natural and social environment so he can intelligently participate in effecting the process of change." I have never seen a better declaration of what a news organization should be, and I believe NPR absolutely achieved that goal. Its strength was in the depth its reporters could provide in five-minute and eight-minute carefully crafted reports containing multiple interviews. That kind of reporting provided context and historical perspective lacking in most broadcast news coverage and even in much of print journalism. I felt my job was to *supplement* that reporting with my interviews, not *preempt* that reporting with hasty chats because FOX was flashing its "Breaking News" graphic again. My last group of NPR bosses felt otherwise.

Then there is the right wing and its blanket labeling of all media except far-right media as "liberal." Most media are mildly annoyed by this but recognize it as political rhetoric. Not NPR. When NPR is called liberal, great angst ensues in the offices of its managers, and protestations are made of the independence and detachment of its journalists. Worse, punches are pulled. NPR allows right-wing criticism to determine what dissenting voices get to be heard and for how long. The more strident critics are passed over. For example, when communications "reform" was proposed in the Clinton administration, it was touted as something that would stimulate competition. Yet it contained a relaxation of rules limiting the number of broadcast stations a single company or individual could hold, almost guaranteeing consolidation of ownership by a few and greatly limiting the number of diverse points of view. I urged that a reporter be assigned to that story or that I be allowed to do an interview about it. After many weeks, I was allowed to do my interview, but it was followed on *Morning Edition* by the commentary of some free-trade tool declaring the "reform" bill would stimulate competition, etc. This was done in the name of balance, but it's the phony balance of having a liar "balance" the truth. The bill passed, and consolidation of media ownership spread to the degree that Clear Channel

Communications ended up owning 1,250 radio station. I suppose Clear Channel believed that *its* competitive situation had been stimulated by the legislation, but what about the rest of the industry? NPR should stop paying attention to right-wing criticism. The badgering of NPR is never going to stop—especially if it's working. NPR should just use its own good judgment, report the facts, and not worry if political partisans don't like it.

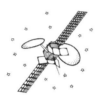

BOBAPALOOZA

After being trashed by NPR management, I had no intention of serving them as a senior correspondent. Judging from the negotiations between NPR's Ken Stern and AFTRA's Ken Greene, NPR didn't want me to be a senior correspondent either. The two Kens were supposed to determine my salary and working conditions for my new job, but they also negotiated severance terms that made it extremely attractive for me to leave the network. Under the agreement, I'd get a generous check if I voluntarily left the company within one year. The amount would be cut in half if I resigned a year later. After that, there would be no payment at all. What could that arrangement be except a mighty incentive to leave NPR? They *really* wanted me gone.

Meanwhile, Andy Danyo was trying to make me see the upside of my firing. I guess she truly believed the old PR person's mantra that there's no such thing as *bad* publicity. She pointed out that the people firing me looked like jerks in the press and that I was looking good by taking the high road and saying all the right things. Andy also had big plans for me, plans that would make her job much easier.

Before the firing, Andy had been planning a three-week book tour to begin in May 2004 with the publication of my book, *Edward R. Murrow and the Birth of Broadcast Journalism*. Her idea of a tour was not just about selling books but also doing publicity for NPR and raising money for public radio stations along the way. Lots of stations wanted me to visit, but Andy had to say no to most of them because I'd only be on the road for three weeks. Then I'd be back at my job on *Morning Edition*. Ah, but now I no longer had a job that required me to be back at NPR in Washington. She could now say yes to all the stations that wanted me to visit, so the three-week tour became the three-*month* tour—the Bobapalooza Tour, she called it.

While I was wrapping up my last month on *Morning Edition*, Andy was making airline and hotel reservations in dozens of cities. It must have been a nightmare of coordination, but she went at it with great enthusiasm. She was enjoying this! She and my publisher arranged a ton of media interviews with newspapers, Bill Moyers, *Fresh Air*, and scores of public radio stations. From a small fifth-floor studio at NPR, I did back-to-back interviews all day for five days before the tour even began.

All these media opportunities were bothering Ken Stern, and he began calculating the possible damage I could do over the next three months in cities all over America—not just publicly in the press but privately in conversations with managers of NPR stations. He made two moves, first summoning AFTRA's Ken Greene for some more lawyerly negotiations. Stern is a guy who thinks you solve a problem by throwing money at someone—buying his silence—then putting some new spin into a press release that the other party is forbidden to refute. Stern told Greene that he wanted me to sign a letter saying I would not sue NPR under the Age Discrimination Act, the National Labor Relations Act, and a dozen or so other avenues that I hadn't even known about. Furthermore, he wanted me to promise I would not speak ill of NPR while on my book tour and handed me a list of talking points I was to emphasize when I spoke.

In fact, they were not talking points at all but rather a horribly insulting set of orders telling me how I was to answer specific questions—and especially how I was not to answer specific questions. I had grown accustomed to being micromanaged at NPR and marveled at Ken Stern's faith in his ability to control the message in all that journalists would write about me on my tour. Here were my marching orders.

You should always speak positively about your past and future career at NPR, emphasizing:

- Your stellar career as a respected journalist and host of *Morning Edition* for nearly 25 years
- The importance of the role you played in moving *Morning Edition* from an alternative news source to the most listened-to morning news program in America
- Your memorable interviews of hundreds of interesting people who have influenced our world, and your style of making them real and human for millions of listeners
- Your future assignments will involve interviewing many more interesting and influential people who have made significant impact on shaping our culture.
- Your having the time to pursue other professional interests, such as writing articles and books, speaking engagements, book tours, etc.
- Your continued support of *Morning Edition* as the number one morning news program, and your continuing to listen to *ME* as your primary news source
- Your belief that public radio is a vital force in this country and is important to promoting public discourse on issues that affect all of us
- Your continuing and enthusiastic support of local public radio stations, as well as the need for listeners to continue to support their stations
- With respect to any questions about the decision to change hosts and the manner in which it was conducted, you should indicate that you have moved on and are looking forward to your new role as Senior Correspondent.
- You should not answer any specific questions about the past actions, other than to say that you have entered into a new phase in your career and plan to be a productive and important voice at NPR for years to come. Wherever possible, accentuate the positives of this change, including freedom to cover the topics of greatest interest to you, opportunity to do long form journalism, more personal freedom to do writing, to develop [your] own work hours, etc. If asked about your salary, you will not discuss whether you make more or less than you did previously. NPR

staff do not discuss their salaries or any other part of their employment package with third parties.

Suggested responses to specific hot topics: Here you will find topical areas that may be brought up by reporters who interview you during your book tour. The responses are not meant to be full, but to give you an idea of what is expected. From these base suggestions, you can modify and expand your answers without going beyond the intended message.

TOPIC   Status at NPR

April 30 is my last day at *Morning Edition*. Then I begin a 3 month book tour. My book is a biography of broadcast legend Edward R. Murrow. When that is over I will begin my new responsibilities as senior correspondent.

TOPIC   Extending to 25th Anniversary

Well, I would have liked that, but you know, I am ready to move on and begin to focus on producing my profiles and really having the time to do the interesting stories I never had the time to do when I was hosting.

TOPIC   The www.savebobedwards.com or its contents

I appreciate the support that listeners are giving me right now. I am sure they are going to continue to support public radio because this is something that is worth supporting. It has to be sustained and the only way that happens is by listeners supporting it.

TOPIC   Volume of letters and e-mail

I have received hundreds of letters from NPR listeners. I am thankful for the kind comments. I am not leaving NPR and I am focusing on the future.

TOPIC   Management's decision about the reassignment

It was a management decision. I am ready to start my book tour and then move on to my new assignment as special correspondent.

TOPIC   What people have said to you in letters and e-mail

Listeners have told me how much *Morning Edition* means to them and how much they have enjoyed my role as host.

TOPIC How will the change affect *Morning Edition*

Listeners will adjust. They will not and should not leave [off] listening to NPR. There's just nothing else on your radio that does what NPR does for you.

TOPIC New job responsibilities

I will be doing in-depth profiles on interesting and influential people that shape our world. I have the room and freedom—and the time—to really do some interesting things. What I like to do are biographies—really getting into the details about what makes a person tick. These profiles will be heard on *Morning Edition* and other NPR Programming.

TOPIC NPR Management

The management of NPR has to make tough decisions. At first I was not happy with the decision, but now I am ready to move on to the next phase of my journalism career.

TOPIC Boycott of *Morning Edition*

I helped to make *Morning Edition* the number one morning news program, and I plan to continue listening to *Morning Edition* as my primary news source.

TOPIC Withdrawal of support to stations

Public radio is vital to this country, and local stations play a vital role in their communities. I urge you to continue to support your local public radio station.

TOPIC Salary

I am not going to discuss details of my salary.

So there were my orders. My reaction, which I didn't share with Stern, alternated between fury at the insult and amusement that he believed I'd actually follow his script. But Stern added a sweetener. In return, I would be paid twenty-five thousand dollars for my silence about NPR's conduct. That was the easiest money I ever made. I had no intention of trashing the organization I'd helped build, but I told Stern through Greene that I would continue to refute their lies about cohosts, 9/11, and my reporting skills. Stern said there'd be no more of that, but there was. I don't think he knew that listeners were sending me copies of emails they'd received from NPR executives parroting the trash Kernis had oozed to the *New York Times.*

A reporter pressed Kernis for the name of a station manager he'd consulted about my "reassignment." Kernis gave him the name of Jane Christo, manager of WBUR in Boston. Christo was furious. Not only had she not been consulted, she opposed my firing and called Kevin Klose to complain about Kernis using her for cover.

NPR tried a new tactic. It told listeners that the reason for my firing could not be divulged because it was a private personnel matter and my privacy needed to be protected. That left listeners with the idea that I must have done something so awful it couldn't be divulged, embezzlement maybe, or exposing myself to the interns.

Perhaps it was desperation that drove NPR executives to a new set of lies that could easily be refuted. The first evidence I got of this was when I visited the Twin Cities on the book tour. *Morning Edition* executive producer Ellen McDonnell had been there just the week before, and according to Bill Buzenberg, who had left NPR for Minnesota Public Radio, McDonnell used every opportunity to slam me. She told Buzenberg than I refused to interview Vice President Cheney because the interview was scheduled for 1:00 PM and I didn't want to stay at the office that late. This was a whopper. The incident in question occurred in 2000, when Cheney was not vice president but a candidate for that office. The interview was not booked for 1:00 PM, but rather 2:30 PM. And, most importantly, I *did* the interview—racking up five hours of overtime that day. My Cheney interview was broadcast on October 11, 2000, and if she'd like, Ellen McDonnell can hear it again on the NPR website. Anyone can. Just two days earlier, *Morning Edition* ran my interview with Texas governor George W. Bush, the Republican presidential nominee.

The NPR board chairman was peddling this same falsehood. Mark Handley was a New Hampshire station manager whom I'd never met, but he presumed to know all about me. In a June 23 email to a listener, Handley wrote that *Morning Edition* sounded so much better without me and that my replacement was interviewing Bush administration officials—"unlike Bob Edwards, who refused to do that." For the education of Mark Handley, I'm providing a partial list of my Bush administration interviews:

Secretary of Veterans Affairs Anthony Principi	3/12/01
Secretary of Education Rod Paige	3/30/01
Secretary of Labor Elaine Chao	4/4/01
OMB Director Mitch Daniels	4/11/01 and 9/13/02
Secretary of Housing and Urban Development Mel Martinez	4/17/01
FEMA Director Joseph Allbaugh	4/25/01
Secretary of Transportation Norm Mineta	5/14/01
FAA Administrator Jane Garvey	7/26/01
Secretary Designate of Homeland Security Tom Ridge	11/16/01 and 11/26/02
Secretary of the Treasury Paul O'Neill	12/4/01
Secretary of Health and Human Services Bill Pierce	1/4/02
Secretary of Defense Donald Rumsfeld	2/14/02
Secretary of State Colin Powell	6/25/02
First Lady Laura Bush	9/17/02
Treasury Department Comptroller David Aufhauser	5/20/03
Secretary of the Interior Gale Norton	6/24/03
Surgeon General Richard Carmona	11/27/03
Secretary of Agriculture Ann Veneman	12/31/03

There were many more, and Mark Handley can hear every one of them at npr.org. So why would the NPR board chairman tell a listener, "Never would you have heard Bob do interviews with top administration officials"? I guess he wasn't a frequent listener of his network's biggest show.

Through Ken Greene to Ken Stern, I promised to file a libel suit against NPR if managers did not refute their own lies and smears. To Greene's surprise, they almost did. Late in the afternoon of the same day Handley wrote his ridiculous email, Dana Davis Rehm, NPR's vice president for member and program services, wrote this to station managers:

> Unfortunately, some people have passed on inaccurate rumors about Bob's departure and I want to dispel these rumors—some of which have proved painful to Bob. First, his departure from *Morning Edition*

had nothing to do with his health, which is fine. Second, some have attempted to tie in Bob's departure to certain concerns about NPR's 9/11 coverage. Again, that is simply not true, and I would remind everyone of the distinguished work Bob and the entire NPR staff performed during this challenging period. To the extent that rumors have persisted that his transfer was based upon his refusal to accept assignments from management, I want to dispel that rumor as well. And finally, Bob did not turn down the co-host position. Bob was never offered such a role.

Never mind that the "some people" passing on "rumors" were managers at NPR—there was my "apology." Unfortunately, it went only to station managers and did not appear in the press, where the falsehoods were planted in the first place. NPR would not make its apology in the press because the press knew where those "rumors" came from. For management to make its confession public would have blown the network's credibility even more.

Ken Stern decided someone from NPR should have me in sight for the whole book tour and report to him on what I was saying. He had in mind a senior staffer in the corporate communications department, but the ranks were thin there. The head of corporate communications, Rodney Huey, was fired as a scapegoat the minute my neatly planned "reassignment" from *Morning Edition* went awry. He was replaced by Jess Sarmiento, who had a small child at home and didn't want to be out on the road keeping tabs on what I was saying. Another woman in the department was about to go on maternity leave, and still another was planning to quit. Andy volunteered for the job and immediately told me about her assignment, making her an instant double agent. She was excited about going with me because she wanted to see her many plans come to fruition. She had organized this tour, and now she could see it through.

Her plan for the tour was brilliant. She told the stations I would do a fund-raising event for them and schmooze with their major donors. In exchange, the stations would rent a theater or auditorium and invite listeners to come and hear me talk about NPR and about my book. Each station would have someone on stage interviewing me about what had happened to me and about Ed Murrow, the subject of my book. Andy provided slides, a brief audiovisual retrospective of my career, and audio clips of Murrow. She even had a script my interviewer could follow if need be. After the interview, there'd be questions from the audience, and then I would sign books. Andy was, as usual, totally organized. She even got an insurance company to pony up some underwriting money for all of this.

Bobapalooza began in Norfolk, then went to my beloved Louisville, where the station manager wanted to name his building after me. Knowing I was going to leave NPR, I told him to delay his idea for three months and see how he felt about it in August. The next stop was New York, and several people in the big town wanted to talk to me about jobs. Before the tour ended, I had twenty job feelers from cable and network TV, public radio, and commercial network radio, and two universities wanted to talk with me about teaching positions. This was all very gratifying after the damage NPR had done to my pride.

Three fabulous musicians turned out for my reading in Nashville—John Hiatt, Marshall Chapman, and Jim Ferguson. Seattle was another high point. There is no better public radio town than Seattle, where KPLU and KUOW are extremely popular, sometimes number one in the ratings. If an NPR host or reporter visits Seattle, there's going to be a crowd. The stations rented a pretty-good-sized hall for my book show, but it wasn't big enough. I had to do the presentation three times in the same place on the same night. I was happy to do it because I sold a lot of books that night and met a lot of wonderful listeners.

We went to Portland, another strong public radio city, and climbed the trails near Multnomah Falls—Andy in heels.

Station KPCC in Pasadena packed a restaurant even though it charged seven hundred dollars to have lunch with me. Among the paying couples that day were Mr. and Mrs. Randy Newman. Speaking to a doctor at my table, Randy said, "All of my friends met their second wives at rehab." He also said Pasadena should have signs all along its border reading Send More Jews.

Santa Cruz was a delight because I shared the bill with NPR's veteran foreign correspondent Sylvia Poggioli and had my first real off-air conversation with her. Sylvia seldom visited Washington, so our talks were always on the air—business, not pleasure. In Santa Cruz, we finally got to talk informally, as real people. Sylvia is one of NPR's big stars. Men have ridiculous fantasies about her; they hear that voice and think "La Dolce Vita!" What they don't know is that Sylvia, while she might be more Italian than a hundred monsignors, is actually from Cambridge, Massachusetts—her parents were scholars at Harvard. I also had the immense pleasure of meeting her husband, Piero Benelezzo, a charming, intelligent, extremely witty and politically savvy journalist.

Andy and I were in Santa Monica on my birthday, staying at Shutters on the Beach, which sent a cake to my room. KCRW had a cake for me too at an outdoor public event. Then station manager Ruth Seymour drove us to the fund-raising event. Ruth is one of the most influential people in public radio and very outspoken about her convictions. In the car, Ruth told me about a conversation she'd had recently with Hugh Panero, the CEO of XM, and how disappointed she was with him. She said she had questions about the viability of satellite radio that Hugh couldn't answer. Internet radio was the future, not satellite radio. Andy and I exchanged glances that said, "She knows—but *how* does she know?" I called Hugh, who said he had not told her. Well, that was just too weird!

Yes, Andy knew I was going to XM because I was I trying to get her to come with me. "We'll see" was the only commitment she'd give me.

Colorado was fun because I reconnected with a couple of longtime and very dear friends—Neil Best, manager of KUNC in Greeley, and Tom Sutherland, a very loyal listener who for six-and-a-half years was held hostage by Islamic Jihad in Beirut, Lebanon.

Two good things happened at Colorado Public Radio. Thanks to a couple of donors, they named one of their studios after me—that was a first. The other thing was a little fund-raising coup. Before a luncheon with major donors, CPR managers told me they'd come up thirty-five thousand dollars short on their capital campaign. I told my luncheon companions about this and mentioned that it presented them with an outstanding opportunity to show how much Colorado Public Radio meant to them. CPR had its thirty-five grand before dessert, plus a pledge for hundreds of thousands more.

In Denver, more than five hundred people packed the fabulous Tattered Cover bookstore, where I was interviewed by CPR's Dan Drayer.

Dan asked, "What have those fifty thousand emails meant to you?" "Everything," I replied, and the audience erupted in applause.

Garrison Keillor invited me to join the cast of *A Prairie Home Companion* for a show at Wolf Trap National Park for the Performing Arts in Vienna, Virginia. I told him I couldn't be part of jokes that would make NPR look bad. He said, "We won't mention it at all. I'll bring you out, the crowd will go nuts, and that's all the statement anyone needs." That's exactly what happened when I did the show. Garrison was a brick.

I spoke in a high-rise church in Chicago. The pastor showed up too. He said he wanted to see what the church looked like when it was filled with people. Later that night, Andy and I had drinks with Tish Valva, a former *Morning Edition* colleague who was then working for Chicago Public Radio. After a few bourbons, I told Tish I was going to XM and asked her to come with me. She didn't hesitate a second.

In Las Vegas, home of KNPR, I was having no luck on the slots, and Andy dropped a quick fifty bucks at the roulette wheel. This was no fun at all. Then Andy got an idea. She had us each get twenty dollars in quarters, which we kept in big plastic beer cups. Then we went to the outdoor patio of an Irish pub and played poker for hours. This was more like it—poker, full glasses, and great conversation about the lark of a trip we were on. She won all my quarters, of course, but she'd earned them.

DENNIS

Then came Boston, on a hot day in June, halfway through our trip. Arriving at Logan Airport, we couldn't find our driver because we didn't know that Logan has a designated place away from the terminal where drivers of limos and town cars wait for their clients. By the time we figured this out, our driver, a large man who weighed at least 280 pounds, had been waiting a long time, sweating in the hot sun.

We headed into town through the Liberty Tunnel and our driver, who'd been talking to his girlfriend on his cell phone, lost his connection. "Damn tunnel," he said, "can't get a good connection." He snapped his cell phone shut, and then he died. Instantly, without struggle or pain—he just stopped living. It happened immediately after he said those words and snapped that phone shut. His head came back onto the headrest and he made a gurgling sound. I thought he had fallen asleep and was snoring, in perhaps the worst-ever case of narcolepsy in the wrong place at the wrong time.

It was the late-afternoon rush hour, and traffic in the tunnel was moving slowly, thank God. Andy and I are forever thankful that this was a one-way tunnel with no oncoming traffic. The town car was drifting to the left. There was a bus beside us in the next lane, and I shouted, "Look out for that bus." Our driver didn't move. The bus stopped as we drifted across its lane. Drivers beeped their horns as we continued our slow drift across three lanes, hitting no cars on our way to the tunnel wall. The wheels were obviously turned a bit left, so that even when we hit the wall, it was only the left front tire that made impact. The car itself didn't get a scratch, but its driver was dead. By this time, I had climbed over the front seat and was slapping the driver, trying to wake him out of his stupor. "Hey wake up!" I was slapping a dead man.

Once we hit the wall and were in the emergency lane at the left of the tunnel, Andy and I climbed out of the car and pulled the driver to the pavement. As I continued efforts to revive him, Andy made a sign reading DOCTOR and held it up, Norma Rae–style, before the oncoming traffic. We got two doctors immediately. As the doctors performed CPR, Andy called 911. They asked for identification, and I looked for the big guy's wallet. His name was John Dennis Bourne, and he was fifty-three years old. He was loaded into the ambulance and taken away. The town car company instructed us to drive the car to our hotel, where they'd pick it up. On the way, Andy learned from the dispatcher that Dennis's girlfriend was blind and diabetic, needing daily insulin shots. Dennis was very important in her life. They had a date to go dancing that night.

TEXAS SHOWDOWN

———

Sharon joined us for the North Carolina part of the tour. Her mother, a North Carolina native, still lived in Mocksville. Sharon brought Sam with her. Sam, named for Samuel Taylor Coleridge, was the Border collie that Sharon added to the family when I got fired and told her she could have a dog. I did my last *Morning Edition* show on April 30, and Sam took up residence on May Day. After I revealed Sam's identity on *Fresh Air*, listeners started bringing dog treats and chew toys to my book events.

During our road show at Fearrington near Chapel Hill, someone in the audience asked about Sam. "Well," I said, "it just so happens that Sam is with us here tonight." When my presentation ended, people filed outside and saw Sharon walking Sam. A buzz went through the crowd. "There he is. There's Bob Edwards's dog." Sam was mobbed like a rock star and absolutely loved the attention.

In Durham, Sam, Sharon, Andy, and I joined a bunch of Andy's old pals for a spirited game of Wiffle Ball fueled by cans of Schlitz and a rainy night at the Durham Bulls' ballpark. Then it was on to Greensboro, an important stop because this was the birthplace of my hero, Edward R. Murrow, the subject of the book I was promoting.

The Murrow place wasn't hard to find, close by Polecat Creek east of Greensboro and at the bottom of a hill. Atop the hill is a Quaker meetinghouse, but certainly not the one where Murrow did his first public speaking. The modern building there undoubtedly replaced the one where Murrow's mother met with other Friends. The old Murrow farmhouse and some of the outbuildings were in ruins and overgrown with weeds. Someone told me the state of North Carolina used to have a roadside marker there but had removed it out of embarrassment over the looks of the property.

I was driving a rental car and caught up with Sharon, who'd pulled to the side of the road to let Sam out for some exercise. When she returned to her car, it wouldn't start. She called AAA on her cell phone, and the guy on the other end was trying to pin down her location. Here's Sharon's end of the conversation as she was looking at a map: "What's the next town on this road? Let's see—it's Climax. . . . No, I'm not *at* Climax, I'm *near* Climax."

The public interviews at these tour stops were almost always fun. In Asheville, North Carolina, I was interviewed by Cleve Mathews, the man who hired me at NPR thirty years earlier. In the Twin Cities, my Minnesota Public Radio interviewer was another ex-boss, Bill Buzenberg, who did not have to ask me how it felt to lose a job at NPR. Scott Jagow was my interrogator in Charlotte. Backstage before the event, Scott asked me about the tour, and I told him what had happened in the car in Boston. That was a mistake. When the public interview began onstage, the first words out of his mouth were, "So, tell us about the dead guy." Classy.

WKNO in Memphis assigned Geoffrey Redick to interview me, and he was a bit miffed about it because it was dumped on him at the last minute. Geoffrey performed a lot better than I did, however. In Memphis, as in other places, a cocktail party preceded the interview. Andy always believed I was more animated in the interviews when I'd had a couple of bourbons beforehand. On this night, Geoffrey had completed the interview and was recognizing audience members for questions. Normally I loved this part of the presentation because I liked interacting with my listeners, but I think Geoffrey noticed that I was increasingly uncomfortable. I couldn't tell him about it in a stage whisper because each of us was wearing a lapel mic and this was something I didn't care to broadcast. Growing desperate, I reached for a cocktail napkin on the little coffee table in front of us. While continuing to answer a question from the audience, I wrote on the napkin, "Will you please wrap this up? I *really* have to go to the gents!" Geoffrey read the note and said, "Well I think we've run out of time. Let's all thank Bob for visiting Memphis." I was offstage before he finished the sentence. Today Geoffrey Redick is a producer for *The Bob Edwards Show*. You have to take care of those who take care of you.

The exchanges with the audience were fun and often went like this:

LISTENER: "Bob, why do you think they pulled you off the show?"
ME: "Well, they said it was to refresh the show to meet the changing needs of the audience."
LISTENERS: "Boo... sssssssssss... boo"
FROM THE BACK OF THE ROOM: "Hey Bob, we love you, man!"
LISTENERS: "YAAAAAAAAY!"

Andy did her duty and made daily reports back to NPR: "More multiple standing ovations for Bob once again in Cleveland—and once again, more booing by the audience at the mere mention of NPR managers." Ken Stern could not have enjoyed getting these reports. Maybe that explains why he played one last dirty trick on me.

The tour was scheduled to end in Austin, Texas, during the last week of July with a speech to the Public Radio Development and Marketing Conference. This was a gathering of the people at public radio stations who raise money—people who had used me for years to pry dollars from donors of all wallet sizes—people absolutely crucial to the health and welfare of public radio. Stern decided I should not keep my appointment.

We were in Idaho in mid-July, the stretch run of the tour, when word was passed to me through Andy that PRDMC had "disinvited" me from its conference in Austin. Why would they do that? I had to know.

The development conference is organized by a company called DEI, whose president is Douglas J. Eichten. Andy got me his number, and I called to ask him why I was no longer welcome at the conference in Austin. Doug sounded honestly confused and replied that he had not disinvited me and that he'd been told I was no longer available as a speaker. In the pause that followed, the light bulb went on for both Doug and me. Each of us had been told a lie. I told Doug that I was

definitely going to be in Austin because I had two other events scheduled there. Did he still want me as a speaker? Yes he did, and we made
it a deal. At last I'd found someone in public radio besides Jeffrey Dvorkin who would stand up to Ken Stern.

The next phone conversation I had was with Stern. Andy had Stern
on her cell phone as she and I pulled up to a private home in Idaho.
We were to attend a party in a donor's backyard. Andy was reluctant
to hand me the phone because she knew what was coming and didn't
want me to be a raving maniac when my job that day was to be nice at
the party. I took the phone and told Ken Stern exactly what I thought
of him. I called him every name except Ken Stern. I didn't care how he
responded because I knew I'd be working for XM just two weeks later.
It was a cleansing "conversation."

The plan was to have XM announce at the beginning of August that
it intended to launch a new channel 133, XM Public Radio, or XMPR,
that would include programs produced by Public Radio International,
American Public Media, WNYC in New York, WBUR in Boston, and
others. The channel would begin in September, and starting October 4,
would feature *The Bob Edwards Show*, produced in-house at XM. All of
this was leaked to the *Washington Post*'s Jennifer Frey so that she could
have a front-page exclusive on the day of the announcement. Unfortunately, another leak altered the plan. When my plane landed in Austin
on Wednesday, July 28, I learned that NPR was reporting that I had a
new job with Public Radio International to do a show that would also
be heard on XM. Okay, so NPR doesn't always get it right, either. By the
end of the day, someone had straightened them out on the story. The
Washington Post story, no longer an exclusive, ran on page A-1 the next
day.

It's very odd that NPR ran a story just as I was arriving in Austin.
Stern didn't want me to speak there because he feared I'd use the conference as a platform for announcing my new job and also reveal all
that NPR had done to me. I had no such intention. So what does NPR
do? It runs a story announcing what it *thinks* is my new job, doing what
it feared I would do.

On that Wednesday night, I called Jay Kernis to resign, with Andy
listening on an extension. I wanted a witness in case my last conversa-

tion with NPR was reported at variance with the facts. After all that had transpired, trust was at a premium.

Kernis made it difficult. Every time I started my little resignation speech, he turned the conversation back to him. He was especially anxious to know how he'd come off in the *Washington Post* story he knew was in the works. Much as he once told me the *Morning Edition* anniversary would be about the future and not about the past, I told him the *Post* story was about me, not about him. He was not resigning from NPR and going to XM—I was. I think he was disappointed. As it turned out, the *Post* made no mention of Kernis whatsoever. That must have killed him.

My speech in Austin went very well. In *Current*, a publication devoted exclusively to public broadcasting, Jeremy Egner wrote, "Edwards capped his last day as an NPR employee with a graceful, funny farewell address." I was shocked to see Ken Stern there—not skulking in the corner either, but right there in the front row—and looking like someone had just shot his dog. Maybe he had some notion of wrestling the microphone away from me if I sullied his name. I was glad he was there. Instead of reading about standing ovations in Andy's reports, he could witness some in person.

The development and marketing directors gave me a handsome award, which I keep in my office today. Perhaps some of the conferees that day knew that Andy and I had raised $1.2 million for sixty-five stations on the tour we had just ended. Then I thanked them "for the best thirty years of my life." I told them that was a long time to bond with an audience and with them. Public radio, I said, was "an ideal I will always support, and I'll continue to visit your stations to help raise money whenever you ask. I'm not leaving public radio. I'm just doing public radio someplace else." Then I left to go do exactly that.

But not before my friends gave me a great farewell party at a Washington hotel near NPR. I even managed to talk my union friend Morgan Fairchild into stopping by to give the party some Hollywood star power. The most touching moment of the evening was provided by one of the shyest people I know. Arthur Halliday Laurent, who engineered most of my *Morning Edition* programs, made a sweetly endearing speech—not an easy thing for Art. He then presented me with the

German-made Neumann U87 microphone I used for thirty years at NPR. I was stunned. Still am. Today it rests atop my parents' 1939 Zenith radio in my living room. It's next to another microphone—a classic Electro-Voice 635A—the very one that carried Red Barber's voice from Tallahassee every Friday for twelve years on *Morning Edition.*

AFTRA

God help the American labor movement, for I am one of its leaders. In fact, for a brief time, I was a union president. I am a proud member of AFTRA, the American Federation of Television and Radio Artists. AFTRA represents actors, singers, dancers, game show hosts, stunt performers, comedians, voice-over artists, models, news anchors, reporters, editors, producers, disc jockeys, announcers, play-by-play sportscasters, meteorologists, and recording artists. Tom Brokaw, Susan Lucci, Norah Jones, Jay-Z, and George Clooney are my union brothers and sisters. AFTRA looks out for the stars, but it's the rest of us who really need AFTRA.

I left NPR after collecting a sizable amount of NPR money obtained for me by Ken Greene, who works in Washington for AFTRA. The big names in broadcast journalism have personal services contracts with their employers that are negotiated by personal agents. At NPR, I had no such star power. I remained close to the lowest-paid NPR news employees by being part of the labor contract negotiated with NPR by AFTRA. So Ken Greene, in effect, is the agent for hundreds of NPR employees. When I got yanked off *Morning Edition*, Ken went to bat for me. NPR made huge mistakes, and Ken Greene took advantage. When NPR smeared me and lied about me, Ken Greene took the matter to NPR's Ken Stern and got me more money. Stern was a formidable foe to Greene when the AFTRA contract was negotiated every three years—

yet now Greene finally had NPR over a barrel and was enjoying himself. He kept coming back to me and saying, "What else have they done? What can I get for you?"

I joined AFTRA in 1972 when I went to work for WTOP in Washington. AFTRA is a strong advocate for its members. Some of us are not very good at negotiating with our bosses for better pay and working conditions, so we need someone to do it for us. That's what AFTRA does. It also unites us with the broadcasters doing similar work at other stations and networks—workers facing similar problems and challenges. If we have a conflict with our employers, we're not alone; we have AFTRA looking out for us.

Gradually I became more involved with AFTRA and ultimately stood for election to the office of first vice president. It's a dangerous thing to be the number-two man in a labor union because you just might happen to be put in charge one day. In 2007, AFTRA's president, actor John Connolly, became the national executive director of Actor's Equity, the union that represents stage actors. This necessitated his resignation from AFTRA and the ascension of the first vice president to succeed him. That would be me, the wrong guy at the wrong time. I was so busy with both daily and weekly radio programs that I had not taken a day off since I left NPR, and I was going to take charge of a labor union? I served as president for about seven weeks and found a way to abdicate in favor of the fabulous Roberta Reardon, an actor who was born to lead our union. She and our incomparable national executive director, Kim Roberts Hedgepeth, led us through one of the most crucial periods in AFTRA's history. Roberta and Kim sacrificed time they wished they'd had for their loved ones and devoted themselves entirely to preserving a labor union serving seventy thousand working professionals.

Today's AFTRA is quite a contrast to the AFTRA of twenty years ago. At that time, we did not have the leadership that members deserved. We were not much of a union at all—actors and broadcasters were at each other's throats. I got involved because I felt broadcasters were not being served by officers or staff members, who were concerned only with the problems of actors. One day we woke up and realized that all of us worked for the same people—Hollywood studios ran the movies, network TV, and the recording studios. Changes were made, and I began to take an interest in the challenges faced by actors and recording artists. The actors began seeing what broadcasters were up against. Today we are a mellow unit acting as one, thanks to far better leaders.

Serving on the boards of three nonprofits, raising money for public radio stations, and being an AFTRA officer are what I do for community service. Roberta and the rest of us on the national board serve without pay. We never really recover all that we spend on travel to meetings, but we don't mind because we believe in an ideal. The essence of a union is that the welfare of the group is more important than the advancement of the individual. I like people who embrace that value. And when I needed AFTRA, it had my back.

XM

———

While on the three-month book tour, I told very few people about my plans because they had to remain a secret. By June, I had to start recruiting a staff, even if it meant risking that the news would leak. At XM, workers were busy converting an employee break room into the office space to be occupied by our program's staff. I had to find an executive producer to work with XM on preparation while I continued to tour. Mark Schramm came to mind because I knew he'd recently left NPR. Years earlier, Mark was the producer in charge of my Friday conversations with Red Barber on *Morning Edition*. After meeting with Kevin Straley, XM's senior vice president for news, talk, and sports, Mark agreed to get the show started. I told Mark that I was bringing Andy Danyo and Tish Valva onto the staff and that I was about to make a pitch to one of my *Morning Edition* producers, Melissa Gray. I suggested other names to him, and I'm sure one of them was Chad Campbell, a onetime *Morning Edition* producer who was then working for NPR's *Talk of the Nation*. Mark made some moves of his own, hiring NPR's Phil Harrell from *Weekend Edition Sunday* and Ed McNulty from *Weekend Edition Saturday*. XM gave us Heather Borthwick, who'd been working for the traffic and weather unit. The XM operations department assigned Sam Wright to our program to take care of all our engineering needs. We were also allowed to borrow the talented producer John Keith whenever we needed him—which was every day.

XM Satellite Radio occupied a nearly-one-hundred-year-old building in a not-yet-fashionable section of northeast Washington, D.C. Our building was a handsome fossil, a onetime printing plant that turned out *National Geographic* long ago. The charming exterior was retained and the guts of the place completely transformed into a home for more than eighty digital radio studios with *Star Trek* appointments. The interior design was part of the marketing pitch: XM was the future. The walls are a photography gallery, bearing huge black-and-white shots of musicians and broadcasters—Kurt Cobain, hair flying, in mid-exhortation; a young Sinatra at the mic; a guitar-strumming Melissa Etheridge, eyes closed and smiling broadly, exhilarated to be performing; the superelegant Duke Ellington and his entire orchestra. We also had Hendrix, Willie, Elvis, Cash, Bowie, Bernstein, Stevie Wonder sharing space with Quincy Jones, B. B. King with Lucille, Janet Jackson on the verge of a wardrobe malfunction, FDR behind a huge bank of microphones, and a baby-faced Orson Welles freaking out the country with *War of the Worlds*. XM was a temple to music and radio.

Either Mark or Kevin led me to the still-under-construction office space of *The Bob Edwards Show*, where some major rewiring was under way to accommodate our computers, speakers, monitors, etc. It's a tight fit for eight cubicles, two offices, and a tiny conference room. Not an inch of space is wasted, but the location is prime—a corner suite looking out in two directions over the capital of the free world. In order to get to our little home, one must pass through a short corridor between two studios. Flanking the entrance to that corridor are poster-sized photographs of the two CBS guys who were the subjects of my books—Red Barber on the left and Edward R. Murrow on the right. That was the wonderful gesture of XM's then-CEO Hugh Panero, who knew how to make me feel welcome. I see those photos every day and think about all three men—Red, Ed, and Hugh.

Phil and Melissa were the first producers to occupy their cubicles, and Melissa was itching to get started on an interview right away. A news interview was out of the question because it would grow stale by October 4, the day for our scheduled debut. Fortunately, there are great musicians visiting XM every day, so our first recorded interviews were with Tift Merritt, Steve Earle, Todd Snider, Mose Allison, and Leon

Fleisher. Walking down the hall one day, I spotted the legendary trio, Peter, Paul and Mary. That was one I didn't need to research—the first concert I ever saw was a Peter, Paul, and Mary performance in Louisville. I coaxed them into my studio and ad-libbed an interview beginning with, "How'd you folks meet?"

Now we had a nice bank of interviews on the shelf, but they were all about music. A couple of *Washington Post* writers helped us out. David Von Drehle was promoting the paperback version of *Triangle: The Fire That Changed America*, and since I'd interviewed David at NPR when the hardback was published, this was another easy one for me. The book is about a 1911 fire at the Triangle Shirtwaist Factory in New York that killed 146 workers, mostly young immigrant Jewish and Italian women. It was a horrific tragedy, but it brought about significant reform and helped empower the labor movement.

I didn't have to go far to find that second *Washington Post* writer, since columnist Eugene Robinson lived four doors from my house. Gene used to cover Latin America for the *Post*, and Cuba is one of his passions. *Last Dance in Havana* is Gene's book about the final days of Fidel Castro's rule and about how impossible it is to separate Cuban politics from Cuban culture, especially Cuban music.

Robert F. Kennedy, Jr., dropped by to talk about *Crimes Against Nature*, his book documenting the Bush administration's destruction of the environment and purchase of scientists willing to write papers supporting Bush policies as environmentally and scientifically sound.

As we collected material, the staff discussed the question "What is this show about?" My answer—"It's about fifty-nine minutes"—was not considered helpful. I was trying to make the point that overdefining the show puts limits on what it can be. I wanted to interview interesting people who would say interesting things. Some producers said that, given my history, the listeners would be expecting journalism or at least a vigorous discussion of current events. No problem, but we didn't have the staff or the resources to be a program that featured breaking news. We settled on this: we would be an interview program featuring people and subjects that interest the host and his producers. Once in a while, we would do a documentary, and whenever possible, we would surprise our listeners. Perfect! That left us with plenty of room to maneuver.

I began our first show on October 4, 2004, by noting it was the forty-seventh anniversary of the first satellite to orbit the earth. Sputnik began the satellite age by sending out an annoying-sounding beep, and here I was starting a new program on a satellite radio system that offered well over a hundred channels of great radio programming.

One of the earliest decisions we made was to have a live conversation on politics with David Broder of the *Washington Post* every week. That gave us some instant respectability. So we knew that David would lead off our first show. Some bright producer pointed out that our debut was to fall on the first Monday in October, the day the Supreme Court begins its new term. So interview number two would be with someone who covers the Court, and we chose Joan Biskupic of *USA Today*. I believe it was Andy who suggested I interview Walter Cronkite as a link to broadcasting's past. I asked Walter if he had any advice for me on our first program, and he replied, "Try to do a second one." The Eugene Robinson interview on Cuba completed our first program. We were on our way.

SATELLITE RADIO

XM Satellite Radio arrived at a time when conventional radio was lacking in imagination and interesting programming. I could sell XM in my sleep because it was that good. It offered 170 channels of programming—80 music channels, most of them commercial-free. It had every nuance of rock, from the hits (Top Tracks) to the "other" cuts you always loved (Deep Tracks). There was a singer-songwriter channel (The Loft) and some alt rock channels. You'd find folk music on The Village and reggae on The Joint, country on America, honky-tonk on Willie's Place, R & B on The Groove, hip-hop on RAW, Beethoven and Mahler on XM Classics, college radio on XMU, children's programming on XM Kids, and dance hits on BPM (Beats Per Minute). There were five Spanish music channels, plus every kind of jazz, bluegrass, and soul music. The lower channels were the "decades" channels—The 40s on 4, The 50s on 5, The 60s on 6, etc.—channels that not only played the music of those particular decades but sound the way radio sounded in each period. When I heard the sound effects and jingles of The 60s on 6, my acne returned.

There were channels devoted to religious programming, comedy, truckers, movies, books, women, and business news. The BBC, C-SPAN, FOX, CNN, Bloomberg, CNBC, and the Weather Channel were all on XM—thirteen news channels in all, including my channel 133, XM Public Radio, which carried *Marketplace, A Prairie Home Compan-*

ion, *This American Life*, and all the public radio hits that were not from NPR. The talk channels covered the whole spectrum from left to right. P.O.T.U.S. politics twenty-four hours a day.

You want sports? XM owned the sports world, and I think its strongest asset was that it carried *every* major league baseball game. Every inning of every game. XM signed an eleven-year contract with major league baseball to secure those rights, and I treasure an email from then-CEO Hugh Panero in which he said I played a role. He said that in making that deal, he was guided by the memory of all those Friday conversations I had with Red Barber. They reminded him that baseball, much more than football or basketball, is a radio game. It is, indeed. XM also had auto racing, ESPN, the NHL, and the PGA Tour. College sports abounded, as we carried the football and basketball games of the Big East, the Big Ten, the SEC, the Pac Ten, and the ACC—also postseason college baseball.

There were many more channels—some permanent and some temporary to allow for maximum flexibility, plus an emergency alert channel for the people who believed the jihadists were looking into our windows.

Truckers and others taking long highway trips loved satellite because they never lost the signal. Drivers and passengers heard the same channel coast-to-coast. If someone changed channels and heard a singer in midsong, he didn't have to wonder who was singing because that information was shared by text right on the radio. It was a user-friendly service.

I wish satellite radio had been around in the 1980s and 1990s because it was badly needed. Commercial radio programming during that period deteriorated, and radio existed mainly as a cash cow for the station owners. It's no coincidence that public radio's audience grew rapidly over those two decades. Listeners longed for an alternative to commercial radio's tired formats, short playlists, rabid talk-show hosts, and incessant advertising. Satellite radio would have thrived during those decades, but you can't rush the future.

In 1992, the Federal Communications Commission allocated a spectrum in the S band for the digital broadcast of radio programs nationwide by satellite. In contrast to the 1920s, when our government gave away the AM band (and later the FM band) to already-wealthy people and institutions, the taxpayers got some money for the sale of any spectrum. Two companies paid $80 million each for a license to broadcast. One was Washington-based American Mobile Radio Corporation, which later became XM Satellite Radio. The other was New York–based CD Radio, later known as Sirius Satellite Radio.

Sirius was expected to be on the air first but was delayed by a chip problem in its radios. XM was set to launch on September 12, 2001. Executives had rehearsed the remarks they'd make at the announcement, and the champagne was chilled for the celebration. Then some planes hit some buildings a day earlier, and no one felt like having a party. XM began programming to Dallas and San Diego on September 25 and then went nationwide on November 12, 2001.

Satellite radio attracted a lot of fine programming talent from across the country—a lot of refugees from stations where the playlists were dictated by program directors who knew more about accounting than music. At XM, the programmers were free to form their own playlists and make use of their considerable knowledge of music and the people who make it.

With my hiring, XM and Sirius went into a battle for what I've always called *programming* but what the Internet-influenced crowd now insists on calling *content*. I think I'm a person, but I've become "content."

On October 6, 2004, just two days after the first broadcast of *The Bob Edwards Show*, Sirius announced it had signed Howard Stern to a five-year contract. One wag at XM suggested I'd have to compete with Stern by doing Stern's kind of content. He said, "Hey Bob, you're going to have to spank some lesbians."

THE BOB EDWARDS SHOW

Friday, November 5, 2004. It was the twenty-fifth anniversary of *Morning Edition*, but NPR listeners heard a most subdued silver anniversary broadcast. Cohosts of six months barely mentioned the importance of that day for a program another guy had hosted for twenty-four-and-a-half years. I mentioned it on *my* show, however, and congratulated Carl Kasell and Ellen McDonnell, who'd been with program since its first day back in 1979.

The very next night I was in Chicago being inducted into the National Radio Hall of Fame. No one from NPR attended the ceremony. I was inducted as an XM guy, though *The Bob Edwards Show* was only a month old.

Being in the Hall, I feel a sense of responsibility to put on programs that will leave listeners feeling I'm worthy of the honor. To do less is to invite mockery: "Hmm, doesn't sound like Hall of Fame material to me!" I've tried to keep my voters from thinking they made a mistake.

I gave my producers a list of people I wanted to interview, and the names fell into four categories: people who'd been very engaging guests for my listeners on NPR, people I'd always longed to interview, people I knew to be capable of sustaining interest for a long period, and old people. Yes, I deliberately went after potential guests in their nineties. Broadcasting covets the eighteen- to thirty-five-year-old listeners, and here I was recruiting nonagenarian guests. This is the beauty of starting a program from scratch and having bosses who left my producers and me free to do the program we wanted. We were (and are) under no pressure to pander to the young. I want young listeners but also middle-aged listeners and the old. I want everyone.

Older guests have the benefit of experience. At the top of my list was actor, disc jockey, and Pulitzer Prize–winning oral historian Studs Terkel (born in 1912). I knew from experience that I could have a full hour of material if I simply said, "How's it going, Studs?" I could discuss the projected problems of the Social Security program with some talking head from a think tank, but I preferred to interview Bob Ball (1914), commissioner of Social Security under three presidents. Arthur Schlesinger, Jr. (1917), worked for FDR and advised JFK. He told me that modern America had too much *pluribus* and not enough *unum*. Negro League baseball star Buck O'Neil (1911) told me how he got the nickname "Nancy"; it was a fifteen-minute story about Satchel Paige, Mrs. Paige, Satch's girlfriend, and a hotel. Stetson Kennedy (1916) had tales of being writer Zora Neale Hurston's boss when both were New Deal government folklorists. That was before Stetson rode the rails with Woody Guthrie and infiltrated the Ku Klux Klan to reveal the Klan's secrets through scripts of the *Superman* radio show. After I interviewed Stets, he married for the seventh time.

Guest John Hope Franklin (1915) has had a most distinguished career as a historian, but he lit up with pride as he recalled doing research for NAACP attorney Thurgood Marshall's *Brown v. Board of Education* case before the Supreme Court. In Hollywood, Bob Mitchell (1912) played organ in silent movie theaters, then formed a boys' choir when the talkies came along. Those are Bob's boys singing with Bing Crosby in *Going My Way*. Writer, producer, and director Norman Corwin (1910), a giant figure of the early days of radio, told me about his V-E Day opus, *On a Note of Triumph*. Ruth Proskauer Smith (1907) cofounded an organization that was one of the ancestors of NARAL, the National Abortion Rights Action League. In Ruth's day, however, the cause was not abortion rights. She and her colleagues were trying to get Massachusetts to legalize contraception for *married* women. Old people have great stories—lots of them.

Do you detect a sense of history? It seems we're never more than three programs away from doing something about history—the New Deal, the Bonus Army, the polio epidemic, and all the wars. We've been big on historic tours from our earliest days, leaving the studio to take listeners to the U.S. Capitol, the National Archives, the National Baseball Hall of Fame, the Museum of the American Indian, the Tenement Museum on Manhattan's Lower East Side, and the homes of Mark Twain and Harriet Beecher Stowe in Hartford, Frederick Douglass in Washington, and the ridiculously opulent mansion of William Randolph Hearst at San Simeon in California, where Victoria Kastner was our guide. We also like art history and went over to the National Gallery of Art for exhibitions of Edward Hopper's work and the national treasures of Afghanistan, which were hidden away during the Taliban era.

As the host of *The Bob Edwards Show*, I can travel now. Since we're an interview show and not a breaking-news show, I can record shows featuring original interviews, then travel somewhere and record more new material for future shows. Producer Melissa Gray enjoyed getting away for interviews in other locations. We went to Oklahoma City for the tenth anniversary of the Murrah Federal Building bombing, to Chicago for a tour of the city's last slaughterhouse and to ask what happened to the old stockyards, and to Missoula, Montana, for a story I especially enjoyed.

Delivering the commencement address at Oregon State University at Bend, I met Debby Barberio, who told me about the annual Italian picnic in Missoula, Montana, where she lived. I was astonished. "You have Italians in Missoula?" Debby gave me a history lesson I'd never heard. When the United States declared war on the Axis powers in 1941, it rounded up all the German, Japanese, and Italian nationals it could locate in the United States and interned them for the duration of World War II. Yes, I knew about the outrageous incarceration of Japanese Americans, but I was ignorant of any imprisonment of foreign nationals other than POWs. Someone in Washington decided the Italians should go to Fort Missoula. Many of those sent to Montana were delighted with their fate. It spared them from having to fight for Mussolini, and they loved Montana. Some of them stayed there after their release, became American citizens, and each year attended Debby's picnic with their children, grandchildren, and great-grandchildren. Debby said if I wanted to talk with them, I'd better hurry because the guys were getting old.

Now *that* is a story made for my show, and Melissa and I (along with our new technical producer, Geoffrey Redick) were off to Missoula to talk with Umberto Benedetti (born in 1911) and Alfredo Cipolato (1913). Alfredo was a waiter working at the Italian pavilion at the World's Fair in New York. One day when he came home from work, the FBI was waiting there to arrest him. At Ft. Missoula, he met a nice Italian girl and went to work for her father after his release. Later, he would run his father-in-law's grocery store. He had just retired when I talked with him, and he fed us some of the last pasta, sausages, and wine that remained on his empty store's shelves. Umberto, who went by "Bert," was aboard an Italian ship in the Panama Canal when the United States entered World War II. The Canal Zone was a U.S. territory in 1941, so Bert, a craftsman and artist, was sent off to Ft. Missoula, where he made many pretty things to brighten up the area where the Italians were held. Like Alfredo, Bert fell in love with America and put down roots. He joined the army, *our* army, and fought in the Korean War. He went to work for the University of Montana and endowed a program in Italian studies.

The interviews with Alfredo and Bert didn't quite make a full program, so we filled out the hour with another colorful, elderly son of Italy. Giovanni Giotta, born in 1920, came to America after the war with nothing more than a desire to get out of a continent devastated by years of war. He landed in San Francisco and became a window washer. Missing the coffee houses of his native Trieste, he opened one of his own once he'd saved enough money. His timing was perfect—the Beat Era was evolving, and the Beats lived on coffee. Today he is known as Papa Gianni and runs the Café Trieste Ristorante. The café is also strong on live music, and it took no prompting to get him to sing for my listeners.

That San Francisco trip was produced by Andy Danyo. Andy and I made another California trip, this time to Los Angeles—and it yielded unexpected gold. It was in LA in 2005 that I did the most satisfying interview of my career.

FATHER GREG BOYLE

Andy Danyo was a radio producer all along—but maybe she knew that. She produced the first two interviews ever heard on our show, simple Q&A's. The real test of a radio producer is in the arts interviews, particularly in music interviews, and in field recording—particularly documentaries. Those interviews turn the producer into an artist. Once I've done my interview, I have performed my particular art. Then I give that interview up to a producer who edits—eliminating questions and/ or answers that didn't work, were incomplete, or interrupted the flow of the story. When appropriate, a producer will add archival audio, a movie clip, or music, and then write an introduction to each segment. In this way, the producers perform their art. I never tell them how to produce it—and I feel very strongly about this. I want my producers to feel total freedom to make whatever they want of my interviews. I respect their talents, and I trust them to use their judgment and do their very best with the material I've given them. They have never disappointed me.

I asked Andy to arrange a trip to Los Angeles so that I could interview Norman Corwin. Completely lost to the current generation, Corwin was *the* dramatic producer-director-writer of 1930s and 1940s radio, able to attract the biggest Broadway and Hollywood stars to his shows. Orson Welles was an early radio legend, but he gladly gave himself up to be directed by Corwin. Andy arranged that interview and produced the hell out of it, but we left LA with an even better interview—one that Andy suggested.

Greg Boyle is a Jesuit priest who works with young Latinos in East Los Angeles. Many of these young people have no responsible adults in their families, so the gangs become their family. Father Greg tries to lure them out of gangs and keep them out. They call him "G" or "G-Dawg." He and his successful ex-gang members become a young person's new family. One of his slogans is "jobs, not jails." To create jobs, he launched a silk-screening operation, a bakery, and a landscaping business. The businesses are now run by the ex-gangbangers, and they're doing well. So is the Homegirl Café, where young Latinas plan the menu, cook and serve the food, and keep the place operating. Andy talked with one of the young women there who was proud that she could now support her daughter, Abcde. She named her child after the first five letters of the alphabet and pronounces it *Ab*-suh-dee.

Homeboy also has an education program teaching life skills, business skills, and financial management. A writing program evolved into Homeboy Press, which teaches desktop publishing, graphic design, typesetting, and Web design and publishes a literary magazine. Homeboy has ten volunteer doctors removing the tattoos that mark these young people for potential assassination if they keep them. Those tattoos are not helpful while job searching, either.

Father Greg says the LAPD has given up on the young Latinos; the cops want the kids in jail or gone. A priest believes in redemption, and *this* priest has seen too many success stories to believe otherwise. It's too easy to see criminals and write them off as flawed human beings. The gang members have heard this so often that they begin to think of themselves that way too. Father Greg sees beyond that and offers motivation for change. He knows they can become positive and contributing members of society if they just get jobs—and he shows them how to do that. He was moved to tears watching a Homeboy baseball game because he saw teammates who were once enemies sworn to kill one another.

I work in Washington, D.C., where politicians proclaim their piety and embrace greedy televangelists to impress their constituents. What's missing is any indication that they've *read* the Bible they're thumping, especially the part where Jesus says the greatest commandment is "Love one another." Then I met Greg Boyle, who has read it and lives it. Refreshing, isn't it? I wish we could clone Father Greg and have one of him in every city.

There was also another angle to the story. Two years earlier, he'd been told he had terminal cancer. His young people were devastated and offered to be organ donors. By the time I talked with him, the cancer was in remission. A guy like that can make you believe in miracles.

Now in my fifth decade of broadcasting, I have interviewed more than thirty thousand people. The interview with Father Greg is my favorite. Five years later, I interviewed him again—another full hour, and he didn't repeat a single story from the first interview. The man is a wealth of great material.

BOB EDWARDS WEEKEND

———

As we entered 2006, executive producer Mark Schramm had moved to another XM post, so Tish Valva moved up to replace him. Tish's former job was filled by Jim Rosenberg. Heather Borthwick took another XM job, so I brought in Shelley Tillman, my former *Morning Edition* colleague. Producer Melissa Gray decided to return to NPR, and Steve Lickteig came over from NPR to replace her. Even with all these changes, I still had a staff who had worked for NPR or its member stations. That's why we were all excited by the launch of *Bob Edwards Weekend* on Public Radio International (PRI) at the beginning of 2006. *Bob Edwards Weekend* consists of interviews that have run on *The Bob Edwards Show*—repackaged in a two-hour format for public radio stations.

We had all wanted to have a presence in terrestrial public radio. With the creation of the XMPR channel 133 back in 2004, XM was already a partner with PRI, American Public Media, and some of the major public radio stations—all the big public radio players except NPR, which had a relationship with our then-rival, Sirius Satellite Radio.

Most local public radio stations carry the national programs distributed by NPR, PRI, and the others. A great many listeners refer to *all* of public radio, local and national, as NPR. So when my voice was heard once again on local public radio stations carrying *Bob Edwards Weekend*, a PRI program, some listeners concluded that I was still at NPR and that NPR's managers had put me back on the air. Oh, the irony!

WESTERN SWING

———

Chad Campbell was the next producer to get ambitious. Chad organized a January 2006 trip to the southern Arizona desert to report on illegal immigration. This was before immigration came up in Congress and set off a real media blitz on the issue, so we were ahead of the pack on this one. Chad, Geoffrey Redick, and I went to the border town of Nogales and rode in a U.S. Border Patrol squad car, interviewing our driver, agent Gustavo Soto, son of a legal Mexican immigrant. We witnessed the arrest of several Mexicans entering Nogales through a storm drainage tunnel that runs under the border. We saw another bust the next day on a second desert drive—this time with the Samaritans, a group of humanitarian volunteers who provide medical assistance to immigrants between Nogales and Tucson, seventy miles north. Our Samaritan driver was Michael Hyatt, a very fine photographer who documented our journey. Dr. Bob Cairns was also aboard; the Samaritan patrols always include a medical professional and someone fluent in Spanish.

We happened upon the arrest of a group so large it required a bus to haul them away. One young man had an ugly head wound, which the Border Patrol attributed to a fall as the migrant was running away. I was doubtful. Dr. Cairns examined him. He clearly needed stitches. I'll never forget the sight of him in his Abercrombie & Fitch T-shirt. Immigrants are advised to wear American gear so they'll "fit in" as locals when they reach the United States.

We did two hours on illegal immigration. The desert ride-alongs were the second hour, and the first hour was an overview of the issue that featured Washington policy makers, activists on all sides, authors, journalists, and, through an interpreter, an illegal immigrant. I loved this story because I can see every point of view that does not involve ethnic hatred and xenophobia. I understand the resentment against lawbreakers, but I also understand the desperation of those breaking the law. Even if they successfully enter the country, these immigrants become a class easily exploited.

"Dangerous Crossings," as we named it, was an ambitious project in itself, but the trip included many additional interviews, several becoming stand-alone shows. We drove over to Santa Fe to interview New Mexico's governor, and later presidential candidate, Bill Richardson. We also did an interview on the Santa Fe arts scene and talked with an opera singer turned innkeeper. Also in Santa Fe, I had the great pleasure of recording an hour with Stewart Udall, who served in the JFK and LBJ administrations as probably the greatest secretary of the interior we've ever had. Landmark environmental legislation was passed on his watch and millions of acres of land protected. Neither of my producers on this trip had been born yet when Udall was in office, so I was happy that Chad and Geoffrey got to learn about him. It probably surprised them to hear that environmental and conservation legislation enjoyed bipartisan support in the 1960s and 1970s. Once Ronald Reagan's supporters took over the Republican Party, respect for the earth was no longer in fashion.

This trip also allowed me to reconnect with an old friend from NPR days. From head to toe, Baxter Black looks like a cowboy. Actually, he looks a lot like the cartoon cowboy on the early albums by the great country-rock band Pure Prairie League. He's even married to a wonderful woman named Cindy Lou. Born in Las Cruces, New Mexico, Baxter Black is a skilled practitioner of art and science hiding inside the persona of a colorful Western caricature. He was once Dr. Black, a veterinarian, who one day realized his stories of adventures wearing a plastic sleeve were getting big laughs. A natural storyteller with a love of language, Bax joined the burgeoning field of cowboy poetry and forged a career so successful that writer Calvin Trillin declared Bax the only person in America who was actually making a living as a poet. Bax likes to play the buffoon—the joke is on him—yet he is also a musician, songwriter, columnist, and brilliant essayist. Of course, he's also a man who hauled an outhouse from his home in Denver to his new home in Tucson, despite both homes having perfectly good indoor plumbing.

After a severe wildfire hit Yellowstone National Park, Bax sent a commentary to NPR. We made him a regular on *Morning Edition*, and he recalls someone on the staff saying we didn't have any other commentators from "out there." Making a fund-raising visit to Denver station KCFR, I had Bax in my audience, and we had some fun at my luncheon speech. Then a snowstorm rolled through and closed the airport. Fortunately, it was Western Stock Show Week in Denver, and since I couldn't leave town, I moseyed on over to the stock show and watched Bax work the patrons in the bar. The man was a performance artist, and the material he was doing wasn't the sweet, all-American wholesome stuff he was doing for NPR. It was closer to the act he did in his frequent appearances on the *Tonight Show* when Johnny Carson reigned there. He had everyone in that bar in the palm of his hand. I was never happier to be grounded by bad weather.

Bax would try to stop by NPR whenever his busy touring schedule blew him into the Eastern precincts, where he felt uncomfortable. On one visit, *Morning Edition* arranged a little nosh for Bax. When the staff did this for some visiting dignitary, the reception usually involved doughnuts and pastries, orange juice, coffee, sliced fruit, and other breakfast fare. Mozelle Stelley, the staffer charged with arranging the breakfast, asked, "Who is Baxter Black?" I responded with the tagline I always used to identify Bax on air: "Baxter Black is a cowboy poet, philosopher, and former large-animal veterinarian." Caterers later delivered celery sticks, carrots, and cauliflower. What's this, Mozelle? "Well, you said he was a former large animal vegetarian."

On this same visit, Bax was buttonholed by Rick Jarrett, NPR's baby-faced, eminently likable computer nerd in the days when all of us were still adjusting to the new technology. Rick got all excited when he spotted Bax. "Hey, you're just the guy I need to talk to. I'm getting married, and I want to take my wife to a dude ranch for our honeymoon. Is there a place you can recommend?" The cowboy summoned his best drawl to reply, "Honeymoon? Hell, son, you don't need a dude ranch. Just get yourself a pair of spurs and check into a Motel 6."

Chad, Geoffrey, and I were wrapping up the immigration story and were about to leave for Santa Fe, but not before meeting Bax for a restaurant dinner in Tucson. After placing our order, we decided to get the bilingual cowboy poet's views on the immigration controversy. Geoffrey, our recording producer, likes to use long shotgun microphones that often provoke amused comment by the guest I'm about to interview. In Baxter's case, our equipment reminded him of his medical days. "The last time I held an instrument like you have in your hand, Geoffrey, I was electro-ejaculating a bull. Miss, where's the men's room?" And with that, he was off to the gents, leaving everyone in the restaurant staring at the three howling Easterners with the funny-looking gear.

HILLBULLIES

The freedom to travel more often and collect interviews inevitably led me back to Appalachia, the land so rich with storytellers. In terms of economic reality, nothing had changed since the 1970s, when I did Appalachian stories for *All Things Considered*. Big energy companies still exploited the region's coal deposits with little benefit to the people who lived there. What *had* changed was the process for extracting the coal.

Industry used to burrow into the beautiful Appalachian Mountains and extract the coal through tunnels. Later it employed the more invasive process of strip mining, cutting away a slice of the mountain all the way around at the source of the coal seam, leaving an ugly scar. Now the companies just take the mountains down. Using a mixture of ammonium nitrate and fuel oil, coal companies blow off the tops and sides of the mountains to expose the seams of coal. The trees, topsoil, and rock are pushed over the side into hollows between the mountains, often burying streams running through the hollows.

Estimated to have formed nearly 300 million years ago, the Appalachian Mountains are North America's oldest. During the last Ice Age, the central and southern Appalachians were spared. When the ice melted, the dense, lush, green forests of Appalachia reforested the rest of the continent. The mountains provide habitat for thousands of species of flora and fauna. The scourge of mountaintop-removal coal mining is the perfect storm of environmental degradation—nature's worst nightmare. It destroys mountains, forests, streams, and habitat all at once. If this were happening in the Adirondacks or the Catskills, people wouldn't stand for it. Here was a story begging for me to return to my home state.

Andy produced it and Geoffrey recorded it. I loved introducing them to my Kentucky friends of thirty years earlier, especially Pat and Tom Gish. Back in the fifties, the Gishes bought the *Mountain Eagle* newspaper in Whitesburg, Kentucky, and transformed it from a weekly account of quilting bees and lodge meetings to a crusading champion of journalism. Tom and Pat shocked local politicians by demanding they hold their meetings in public, as mandated by law. Editorials about nepotism in public school hiring caused quite a stir. Coal companies, which controlled everything in the region (and still do), could not believe that a local newspaper would challenge their authority. There was pushback, of course, first in the form of an advertising boycott. When that didn't work, the paper's office was set afire. A Whitesburg city police officer was convicted of the crime. Nothing stopped the Gishes from doing their journalistic duty. There are a lot of big-city publishers who are not nearly so bold as Pat and Tom, who saw the subjects of their editorials every day at the coffee shop and the grocery store and at church on Sunday.

Tom Gish was part of our documentary, as was a nature scholar, a county official, and people whose quality of life had been destroyed by mountaintop-removal coal mining. The principal spokesperson for the industry was Bill Caylor of the Kentucky Coal Association, who touted coal as our cheapest and most abundant source of energy. He reminded us that more than 50 percent of the nation's electricity is supplied by coal-burning power plants and that we need cheap fuel to power our computers, refrigerators, and air conditioners. The cost in dollars is cheap, but I had plenty of witnesses to other costs, including the loss of mountains, forests, streams, and a way of life.

Our star was writer Wendell Berry, whose essays on community are world-renowned. When Wendell pronounced mountaintop removal a "sin," I could already hear the closing music swelling in the background. I wrapped it up by noting that the process enjoyed bipartisan support (Kentucky's two Republican senators and West Virginia's two Democratic senators accept political dollars from coal companies).

I also mentioned that even the country's major environmental groups did not list the end of mountaintop-removal coal mining as a top priority because they're so focused on global warming—the reigning popular environmental cause. It's great that they're concerned about the burning of coal, but maybe they should also take a look at how the coal is obtained. We called our documentary "Exploding Heritage" to make the point that it's more than mountains being destroyed.

Chad did some polishing to Andy's production, and Geoffrey did a lot more than hold the microphone for my interviews. Against his better judgment, he went up in a small plane to record my aerial observations of the massive destruction of the region. He braved lightning during a thunderstorm to record a mine site explosion. Geoffrey stood by the side of an Eastern Kentucky road to get the sound of coal trucks rumbling by, and with heavy audio gear strapped to his back, he ran across a field thick with briars and brambles to get to a spot when a coal train was about to pass. The train's engineer spotted him and obliged with a robust whistle blast.

The payoff we desired for our efforts was the end of Big Energy's destruction of Appalachia. The blasting continues, however, reducing ancient forested mountains to treeless mesas sprayed with seeds of some wild nonnative grass. Industry touts the flattened land as an opportunity for economic development, but the reshaped earth has some settlement issues. A Wal-Mart built on one of these sites now has a cracked foundation. Likewise, a prison built on another site slipped deeper into the dirt, so critics have dubbed it "Sink-Sink." Coal companies are proud to proclaim the wonders of a golf course built atop some former mountains. Surely the links are a comfort to people living in one of the poorest regions in America.

We get our electric power by abusing the powerless. How is it that a region so rich in a valuable natural resource has some of the worst schools and poorest health care in the nation? Perhaps the absentee owners of the energy companies should be required to establish a neighborly social contract with the people whose land they've trashed.

But it's only Appalachia. Congress blocks oil drilling in Alaska's Arctic National Wildlife Refuge where no human lives, but it supports the rape of Central Appalachia, home to 7.5 million people.

THE INVISIBLE

Some years ago, Andy introduced me to her friend Jamila Larson, a social worker in Washington, D.C. Jamila has seen the worst that a big city can do to people without resources or family to get them through hard times. Most of her stories are heartbreaking, but one was so amazing and uplifting that I knew I had to get it on the radio. Jamila said there was a homeless teenager who lived on the streets of Washington and slept in Union Station, a short walk from the U.S. Capitol building, an iconic symbol of our nation's greatness. The kicker was that the kid was headed for Columbia University even though he hadn't been in a classroom since he was twelve years old. That's more than an interview; that's the seed of our next documentary.

Early in 2007, I asked Andy to have Jamila give us all the particulars and we'd get started on production, but Andy had other plans. She was moving to Pittsburgh and couldn't produce a documentary from there. She refashioned her job and would now research, book, and prepare my interviews, but, lacking access to the editing programs in the XM computers, she could not do postinterview production.

To make matters worse, we already had a producer opening. One of the applicants for the spot was Ariana Pekary, whose sample production CD included an interview with a homeless man in Washington, D.C. Hmmm. I was very subtle when she arrived in the office. She said, "Hi. I'm Ariana." I said, "Hi. I'm Bob, and I'd like you to produce a documentary about homeless children." In just a month or two, Ariana, Geoffrey, and I were on the campus of Columbia University interviewing young Thomas Healey.

Tom makes an immediate impression. He's what your grandma would call whip-smart. His acceptance at Columbia testified to his academic smarts. The *street* smarts he needed to get from ages twelve to eighteen—alone in this cold, hard, predatory world—are harder to come by. Most of us never would have made it.

Tom said he had been living a comfortable middle-class life in Austin, Texas, until his single mom developed schizophrenia and lost her small business. He could not turn for help to his father, a drunk who was killed when he wandered into the path of a speeding car. "I suddenly realized that I was the grown-up in the family," he told us. Tom was just twelve years old when his mother got sick, but he knew what would happen if she were institutionalized. He was the first of many young people to tell me they had heard all the horror stories about foster care and were not going to be its victims. He decided that he and his mother should leave Austin and take a bus—first to St. Louis and later to Washington. In both cities, he found places that would accept his mother. Shelters and institutions that care for women do not allow males over the age of twelve to live with women. Male shelters, according to Tom, are death traps for boys, so he could either accept foster care or live on the street.

There's nothing heroic or romantic about survival in Tom's old environment. He shoplifted, panhandled, hustled, sold his body, and dealt some drugs—things he felt he *had* to do to get by. He's not proud of it—but there it is. At least his record is clean; he was never caught. "You must have been pretty good," I told him. "Lucky, not good," he replied.

He learned where the unoccupied houses were and how to break in to them. The night he spent in a high school gym was the only time he went to school after dropping out of fifth grade. But he was smart enough to hold some legitimate jobs while homeless. After two weeks of working at a camera store, he was *running* the camera store. More incredibly, he worked at a bank. Does anyone check references anymore? Imagine people getting financial advice from a homeless teenager.

Ultimately, Tom encountered Gina Kline, who was then working with a nonprofit group trying to find jobs and services for the homeless. Impressed with Tom's intelligence, she urged him to get his GED certificate and give college a try. Tom asked Gina where she went to college. "Columbia," she said. "Okay, I'll apply there." From a makeshift bed near the bike rack at Union Station, Tom Healey entered the Ivy League. Tom loved it there, but his waiter's salary and tips couldn't cover tuition and rent. For his sophomore year, he was back in D.C. at George Washington University on full scholarship.

Then I interviewed Tom's female counterpart. Carissa Phelps also became homeless at age twelve. She complained to her mother about her stepfather's sexual advances. Mother Dearest decided she needed her husband more than her daughter, so she drove Carissa to juvenile hall in Fresno, California, and told her to get out. Juvenile hall wouldn't take her in because she hadn't done anything wrong, so Carissa slept in the doorway for several days until a man introduced her to the world of child prostitution. That was her life for the next six years until, like Tom Healey, Carissa met the right social worker who urged her to get her GED. Also like Tom, Carissa had skipped grades 6 through 12. I'm really beginning to question the value of those grades, because when I interviewed Carissa, she had just added a law degree to the MBA she had earned at UCLA.

Ariana and I knew the stories of Tom and Carissa were ridiculously atypical. Most homeless kids fare miserably. I interviewed Rick Koca, founder of an advocacy group called Stand Up for Kids, and he told me an average of thirteen homeless children die each day. Rick also told me that a lot of the homeless teenagers are gay and lesbian, thrown out of their houses by parents who can't love a child who's not heterosexual. That was a shocker for me—that parents would disown their own kid for not fitting their image of the ideal child.

Producer Dan Bloom handled the recording duties and joined Ariana and me for a visit to the Sasha Bruce shelter for homeless teenagers in Washington, D.C., where we found kids who'd been terribly abused by the people who by law and morality were supposed to love them and care for them. Our first appointment was with a uniformed young woman who'd just finished her day at military school. I said simply, "Tell me your story." She was silent. Then tears formed, followed by gasps, and then sobs. Her "story" had formed in her brain and apparently brought back horrors she didn't care to share. I felt terrible, apologized profusely, and left her in the arms of a consoling staff member.

Seven others volunteered to tell their stories of parental abuse and homelessness. These were escapees from parents or stepparents. At least two of them were parents themselves—"babies having babies," as Jesse Jackson famously described them, and already behind the eight ball before they could vote. They may never climb out of the situation they're in. One young man absolutely broke my heart. He talked about his determination to make it in the world and wanted to show us his closet. I pressed on with my interview, determined to get his story and totally uninterested in his closet. This guy believed in a dream—he was going to make something of himself, yet everything he was telling me—and the way he was telling it—convinced me that he was not going to score points at any job interview. Finally, I relented and had him lead us to his closet. It was the picture of military neatness, and this young man had somehow managed to spend a small fortune on clothes. There were sport coats and dress shirts in a rainbow of pastels. What really got to me were the shoes. On the closet floor, arranged like little soldiers, were about two dozen pairs of shoes, and absolutely every pair were sneakers. He had judged the worth of the shoes by their expense and not by appropriate style. It had not occurred to him that grown-ups in the business world do not wear sneakers.

I had mixed feelings about the rest of my interviews at the Sasha Bruce House. I felt good that we were getting stories more typical of homeless teenagers to balance the unlikely success of Tom and Carissa, but I felt awful about the fate of these African American kids. They were determined and lovable but badly scarred and perhaps doomed. Then the last one walked into the room and completely lit the place up.

Smart, sassy, and entertaining, Zanoni Bishop told me her story about a schizophrenic stepmother who clobbered her over the head with a vase. Zanoni left home and started couch surfing, staying at the homes of various friends. Then she slept in the park. She told me that she "always went to school—no matter if I was hungry or filthy, I'd always go to school." Then she mentioned Advanced Placement courses, and I had to break in.

> ME: Okay, just to backtrack here. You are drifting between friends and the park and you're taking AP courses?
>
> ZANONI: Yes, AP world history, AP U.S. history, AP lit, and AP chemistry.
>
> ME: Where are you doing all this homework?
>
> ZANONI: Oh my God, like, you have to do your homework before the sun goes down, because if you don't, then you're going to have to do it by the streetlight, and your eyes are going to start aching. If I get it done outside, under the sunlight, that's cool, but the English lit class was hard because you've got to read a lot, and you don't even just have to read, you have to *critically* read. And then the chemistry class, this was, like, hard because I'm the worst at math.

I asked her if she was on track to graduate. She said she had a 3.7 GPA but wanted to take some more courses to raise it. Then I asked her what she wanted to do in college. Her response: "I want to do international business with a minor in linguistics first, then I want to do international law, and then I want to do mass communications. I want to take it step-by-step because my main, my core interest is emerging economies, like Brazil and Latin America. They have, like, their rain forest is holding the cure to everything. So if I can, like, affect laws that are being made in terms of how they're treating this environment, then at least I can make that little, little difference."

Okay, here's a highly motivated, attractive, African American female with a 3.7 GPA—and she's homeless. I was thinking that if there's no scholarship for Zanoni, then the whole concept of affirmative action is bogus. She must have found that scholarship, because the last we heard of her, she was heading for Florida A&M in Tallahassee, home of the Rattlers.

"The Invisible—Children Without Homes" aired in the closing days of 2007. I figured rookie producer Ariana Pekary had done just about the best program she could do, but I was wrong because she went out and topped it.

3ᴿᴰ MED

One of my listeners wrote me an email in January of 2008.

DEAR BOB: My name is Al Naar. I served as operating room corpsman with the 3rd Medical Battalion during the Vietnam War. On May 2 & 3, 2008, in Charleston, SC, the officers and men of 3ʳᵈ Med will assemble once more . . . and hold their 40 year reunion. . . . There will be over 100 doctors and corpsmen who served together and will see each other for the first time since leaving Vietnam 40 years ago. This presents a rare and unique opportunity to interview surgeons who left private practice, joined the military and served during a difficult time in our nation's history. There are many stories that came out of the Vietnam War. However, very little if any have ever been recorded of the extraordinary service of these individuals. As an avid listener to your show, I feel that this subject matter would be compelling and of interest to many in your audience.

I thought so too, and so did Ariana. The battalion served in several field hospitals close to the DMZ. What these medical men were dealing with in 1968 were the results of a double whammy: the siege of the U.S. Marine base at Khe Sanh, which began on January 2, and the Tet Offensive, launched on January 30. Think of M*A*S*H, with the wisecracks, the black humor, the irony of sewing up men so they could go back to an unpopular war and risk their lives again, the antiwar feelings of some of these military officers at war, the music playing in the operating room—3rd Med had all that going on too, except these were navy doctors serving on land. Their patients and their corpsmen were U.S. Marines. If there were still travel funds in the budget by May, we'd be going to Charleston.

Then I checked my calendar and was horrified to see that I was already booked for that weekend. I was to deliver the commencement address at the University of St. Francis in Fort Wayne, Indiana. As much as I wanted to go to Charleston, I didn't want to break my commitment to USF. So Ariana went alone to 3rd Med's reunion. From Fort Wayne, I sent her a text message: "Getting anything good there?" She replied, "If you call making grown men cry—good, yes." I answered that she'd been doing that for many years.

What Ariana recorded in Charleston was solid gold. We called the program "Stories from 3rd Med—Surviving a Jungle ER." I spoke very few words—identifying a speaker now and then. The men told their own stories. Dr. John Munna, a trauma surgeon from New York, described operating on his first case in Vietnam as the hospital was under fire. He also did bare-handed heart message on a marine, commanding him to "Live, live—don't you die on me." Dr. Norman Pollack spoke of the most horrendous cases, victims of booby traps, phosphorous (which continues to burn and can't be put out, so it must be *cut* out), and Bouncing Bettys, land mines that pop up to a height of five feet and decapitate people. He also told of doctors who couldn't deal with what they were seeing and had to be reassigned.

There were no defibrillators available to 3rd Med, so Dr. Jack Hagan and corpsman John Little fashioned one from a pair of kitchen knives, an electrical cord, and a generator. Little recalled a marine wounded while clearing a minefield. He was hit in the head, eyes, heart, and belly. After surgery, he said he was to be married in two weeks. When told he was blind, the patient said he didn't want to live anymore. Then he died.

On the first day of the siege of Khe Sanh, twenty-six-year-old Dr. Ed Feldman was assigned a marine patient who had "what looked like a pipe" extending from his abdomen. That "pipe" was actually an unexploded 82-millimeter enemy mortar shell. The hospital had been under attack and had no power. Dr. Feldman operated with marines holding flashlights over his patient. A sergeant advised him as to which parts of the shell he could touch. The doctor and the marines were all standing behind sandbags in case the shell exploded. The patient knew nothing of all this until he arrived in the Philippines and the press corps was waiting to interview the "human bomb." He, the flashlight-holding marines, and Dr. Feldman are all alive to tell this story today. I learned something else about Dr. Feldman from Al Naar, who visited us at XM one day while Ariana was still putting her show together. Al told me that sometimes there'd be no corpsmen available to go out to the battlefield to pick up the wounded, and on those occasions, Dr. Feldman would grab a helmet, jump aboard the chopper, and go do the work of an enlisted man. As a former grunt, I found that almost as impressive as his surgical live-mortar extraction in the dark. Dr. Feldman was awarded the Silver Star. I think he deserved more.

The doctors were amazing. Some had contacted the parents of patients they'd lost, and some had visited the Vietnam Veterans Memorial in Washington to find on that great black wall the names of boys they tried to save. It had all happened so long ago, yet they were telling young Ariana that it felt like it was only yesterday.

Al Naar said there should be music in the show because 3rd Med had music in its OR, just as Hawkeye and Trapper John had on M*A*S*H. Ariana asked me for some ideas. So punctuating all these compelling stories of life and death forty years ago were Neil Young, Bob Dylan, the Doors, and Crosby, Stills, and Nash. We don't usually do documentaries with a sound track, but Al Naar was right and it worked.

Listener response to the program topped anything we'd done before. The note that really got to us was this one:

> I listen every day to the show while delivering mail, and when I heard this I had to pull over and weep. If I had heard this years ago, I might have understood just a little better what the man who is now my ex-husband had undergone during the year he was in Vietnam. Dr. Munna treated him when he was wounded in May 1968. It was obviously still so much with all who were interviewed; it almost sounded as if they must be veterans of this current debacle. And while I wept for the men who told their stories, I fear for the spouses and sweethearts and, yes, the

children of those men and women who are enduring these terrors today. How much will the misery be multiplied, and what can ever be done to mitigate the pain? Tonight each of these people are in my thoughts and prayers. Thank you, thank you for bringing us such a moving program. And Craig, I'm sorry I never REALLY understood.

—LORNA

Yes, Ariana made grown men cry—women too, according to Lorna—and on the day the program aired, Ariana made one more grown man cry. I listened to the program in my office and then went to her desk to congratulate her. I told her that I got into radio in order to make programs like that one, and then I was in tears. She said, "Me too," and now she was crying because I was. Okay, this was awkward, so I went outside and had a smoke.

NOLA

My producers got even more ambitious in 2009. Ariana Pekary continued her run with a documentary show called "Hating Marcelo." This was about hate crimes against Latino immigrants. Marcelo Lucero was thirty-seven years old when he was killed by seven teenagers in Patchogue in Suffolk County, New York. "Beaner hopping" is apparently a popular sport for bored Long Island high school boys who've had a few beers. Lucero had been a productive worker in his community for longer than his attackers had been alive. The local county executive used the immigration issue to increase his popularity with the masses and was a frequent guest on CNN of Lou Dobbs, who was also fanning the anti-immigrant flames in his quest for ratings. We wondered if the teenagers felt they had official license to commit violence against Latinos.

Ariana scored again with a five-part series on education reform that was largely instigated by me. I remain convinced that private industry sees public education as the next great profit center ripe for the picking. I believe corporations want to take it over in the same way they absorbed hospitals and nursing homes that were once run by government and religious institutions.

Producer Dan Bloom jumped into the pool with a program on Iraqi immigrants in America. And in 2010, Dan did some reporting from South Africa, where he was enjoying soccer's World Cup.

There was also a five-part series on the future of the printed book in light of modern computerized technology and the introduction of so many new electronic devices. Cristy Meiners was the principal producer of that one, though I think all ten of us got deeply involved in it in one way or another. We are people who love books working on a program that celebrates writers. Whatever delivery system publishing chooses, *The Bob Edwards Show* will be aboard.

Next came the most ambitious project in the history of our program. Producer Chad Campbell asked me if I wanted to go to New Orleans, where he was born. Well, who in his right mind passes up a chance to go to New Orleans? Our target was the 2010 Jazz Fest, a local heritage festival that attracts many thousands to the Crescent City—a celebration of the music New Orleans spawned and which keeps it a valuable national asset. Memphis-based Geoffrey Redick filled out our trio—a reunion of the team that produced two hours on immigration in the Arizona desert, toured the Baseball Hall of Fame, and covered a launch of the space shuttle Endeavour. We came back from New Orleans with a dozen interviews with some of America's most amazing musical talent—Allen Toussaint, Dr. John, Anders Osborne, Theresa Andersson, Trombone Shorty, Stanton Moore, Jon Cleary, Irma Thomas, Roger Lewis of the Dirty Dozen Brass Band, Ben Jaffe of Preservation Hall, Jimmy Carter of the Blind Boys of Alabama—and by the time we got to the fabulous jazz chanteuse Keely Smith, it was obvious I had picked up some serious crud on the flight to the Big Easy. I sounded terrible interviewing a singer known for her perfect tone and enunciation. When I got back home, I was even worse. My doctor treated me for pneumonia, and I was in a hospital for three days. Still, we were making plans to go back.

The BP oil platform explosion had occurred just before Jazz Fest, and people knew the leaking oil would seriously damage the coastal wetlands so vital to the protection of coastal Louisiana, including New Orleans. So in early July, we returned to the Gulf Coast to talk with scholars, reporters, oystermen, shrimpers, duck hunters, doctors, conservationists, and anyone else with some expertise on the coastal wetlands, the BP spill, and the entire history of oil drilling in the Gulf of Mexico. We were also nearing the fifth anniversary of Hurricane Katrina and asked people to assess the health and well-being of New

Orleans in the wake of two major disasters. Our goal was a pair of one-hour documentaries—one on BP and another on the Katrina anniversary. Once we collected the material, we changed our minds. The interviews were just too good to break up into documentary sound bites. Instead, Chad and Geoffrey produced seven one-hour programs for a series called "No Place Like Home."

We ran the music interviews on nine consecutive Wednesdays in June and July, then followed that with "No Place Like Home," also on Wednesday. So for sixteen consecutive Wednesdays in the summer of 2010, our listeners heard about southern Louisiana—and most loved it.

EPILOGUE

In July 2008, XM was absorbed by its rival to create Sirius XM Radio. The Federal Communications Commission had taken a year and a half to approve the merger, but despite that period of uncertainty, the staff of *The Bob Edwards Show* remained stable. In fact, the show matured during that time and was finally over its initial shakedown period. This had a lot to do with the leadership of executive producer Steve Lickteig. Steve appointed Ed McNulty as senior producer for our daily show and Chad Campbell as senior producer for our weekend show. Steve also hired producers Dan Bloom and Cristy Meiners. *Bob Edwards Weekend*, which began with a dozen stations, now has 150. We are operating smoothly and doing the best work we've ever done. Our new bosses are just as supportive as their XM predecessors were, so all of us on the show are committed to making Sirius XM the success it deserves to be.

Good fortune has blessed me twice with the same opportunity. I got to join NPR in its third year when it was still bold and experimental and had only a million listeners. When I left thirty years later, it had well over twenty million listeners. I enjoyed the same stroke of luck when I joined XM in 2004 when it had only a million subscribers. As of this writing, the combined Sirius XM has more than twenty million subscribers. It is tremendously exciting to be part of something new and ask the questions "Can we make history here? Can this start-up break new ground in radio?" I know from both experiences that the answer is yes. Sirius XM has the potential to be the radio choice of perhaps fifty million Americans, and I'm working to help make that happen.

I love my show, and I believe it's the program I was always meant to do. The interviews are important records of the opinions, dreams, and many achievements of the extraordinary people who have been my guests; I want those chats preserved somewhere in an archive accessible to all. It's a program about values and ideas and ideals. We've tried to expose what's wrong but also to celebrate what's wonderful and inspiring and beautiful.

The Bob Edwards Show has won national journalism awards, the first ever for satellite radio, and it has demonstrated that there's a place for public affairs programs produced in-house. We have the capability of offering the kind of public radio Bill Siemering envisioned in 1970 that would "celebrate the human experience as infinitely varied rather than vacuous and banal." As we've already shown, documentaries of original reporting are well within our scope.

The show is still very young, but it's already taken me to snowy Montana, desert Arizona, swampy Florida, gritty coal sites in Kentucky, a slaughterhouse in Chicago, Cajun bayous, the historic Dakota apartments in New York City, homeless shelters in Washington, D.C., the opulent Hearst Castle, stunning Big Sur, the barrio of East LA, the Baseball Hall of Fame, a still-mourning Oklahoma City, the Hartford homes of Mark Twain and Harriet Beecher Stowe, the Lower Ninth Ward of New Orleans, an army post in Kansas, the National Gallery of Art, and a happy coffeehouse in San Francisco.

My children are grown and gone. Brean, married to Anna, works for Cisco in California. He is a graduate of Clemson University. They have a daughter, Jerdahn. Susannah, a Phi Beta Kappa graduate of Goucher College, earned an MFA at the Savannah College of Art and Design, teaches art in the Fairfax County, Virginia, public school system, and longs to be a professional illustrator. Eleanor, a three-year magna cum laude graduate of Marymount University in Arlington, Virginia, is working in the retail food business in Winter Park, Florida. Their mother lives on a twenty-two-acre farm in Virginia with my ex-dog Sam. I am learning how to be alone.

It might be too early to write about my life, because I know there are exciting and probably challenging chapters ahead. I feel I'm still growing as an interviewer and that my best programs are yet to come. I'm writing this at the happiest period of my professional life, a time when it's a joy to go to work and learn new things from my guests and from my young and talented staff. To see those young producers challenge themselves, take on special projects and documentaries, and be successful at it is a source of great joy for me. I hope it continues for a very long time because I'm having too much fun to give it up.

One of my favorite movies is *Broadcast News*, in which William Hurt plays shallow but handsome TV anchor Tom Grunick and the marvelous Albert Brooks plays the smart but less-flashy reporter Aaron Altman. Grunick says to Altman, "What do you do when your real life exceeds your dreams?" Altman replies, "You keep it to yourself." That's clever Hollywood writing, but that's not what you do. What you do is dream new dreams—and I'm working to make my new dreams come true.

INDEX